QUILTINGBeauties

Come in All
Shapes &
Sizes

Karen Neary

American Quilter's Society
www.AmericanQuilter.com

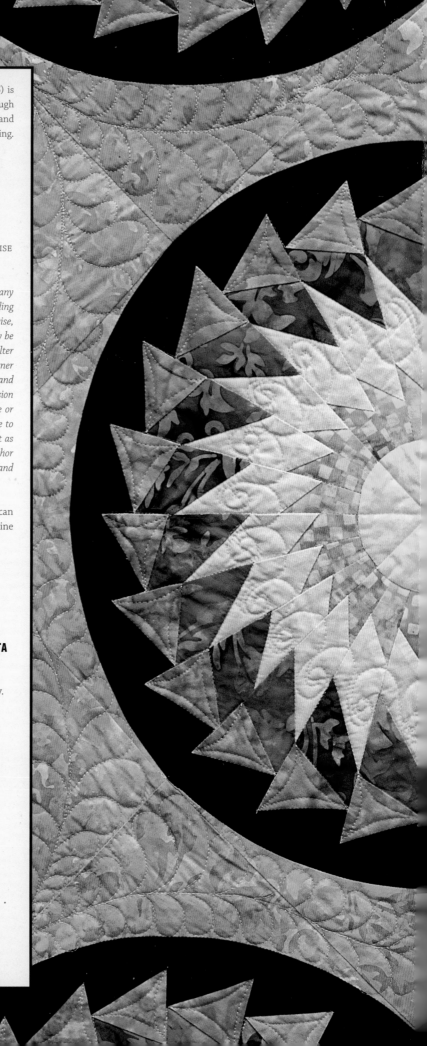

Located in Paducah, Kentucky, the American Quilter's Society (AQS) is dedicated to promoting the accomplishments of today's quilters. Through its publications and events, AQS strives to honor today's quiltmakers and their work and to inspire future creativity and innovation in quiltmaking.

EXECUTIVE BOOK EDITOR: ELAINE H. BRELSFORD
BOOK EDITOR: KATHY DAVIS
COPY EDITOR: CHRYSTAL ABHALTER
GRAPHIC DESIGN: ELAINE WILSON
COVER DESIGN: MICHAEL BUCKINGHAM
HOW TO PHOTOGRAPHY: KAREN NEARY
QUILT PHOTOGRAPHY: CHARLES R. LYNCH, UNLESS OTHERWISE NOTED

Additional copies of this book may be ordered from the American Quilter's Society, PO Box 3290, Paducah, KY 42002-3290, or online at www.AmericanQuilter.com.

Text © 2014, Author, Karen Neary
Artwork © 2014, American Quilter's Society

LIBRARY OF CONGRESS CATALOGING-IN-PUBLICATION DATA

Neary, Karen.
  Quilting beauties come in all shapes & sizes / by Karen Neary.
    pages cm
  ISBN 978-1-60460-164-0
  1. Patchwork quilts. 2. Quilting. I. Title.
  TT835.N355 2015
  746.46--dc23

                        2014044641

Dedication

This book is dedicated with love to Beryl Sutton of Truro, Nova Scotia— friend, mother, mentor, and my constant support. Mom called daily to check on the progress of the quilts for this book and to offer encouragement for its completion. Sadly, my mom passed away before it was finished; there are two quilts she did not get to see. I know she would have been so proud to hold this book in her hands. I love you, Mom, and thank you for always being my biggest cheerleader.

Acknowledgments

None of us can do it all by ourselves; we are part of a team and my family members are definitely Stanley Cup contenders. I am blessed to be married to my best friend, Jamie. For over 30 years he has endured, encouraged, and enthusiastically enabled all things quilting. Being as handy as a pocket in a shirt, he is always there to do what needs doing—from building racks and frames (or whatever I fancy on a particular day!), lugging supplies to and from workshops, helping with photography, and locating quilt shops while travelling.

I appreciate the contributions of my two sons, Patrick and Peter, who are quick to offer opinions on color, composition, grammar, and mathematical enigmas, and who come up with clever names for many of my creations.

My brother, Lawrence, offers encouragement from the sidelines, while my sister, Nancy, takes the time to check my quilt tops before they are basted. She always finds a polite way to say, "Do you know you have a block upside down?"

I am ever grateful to Gram, the late Myrtle Patterson Davis of Five Islands, Nova Scotia, who started me on the path to quilting and whom I remember fondly as being able to do anything she set her mind to. What a role model!

A profound and sincere thank you to pattern testers Lynn Bourgeois of River Philip, Nova Scotia; Darlene Gerber (I Quilt Scarlet and Gray at iquiltscarletandgray.blogspot.com) of Geneva, Ohio; and Kari Lippert of Hanover, Maryland. I cannot thank all of you enough for your generous investment of time and talent in helping make the instructions in this book as clear and precise as possible. I offer hugs and a huge round of applause for a job well done to each of you.

Thanks to Beth Munroe of Mrs. Pugsley's Emporium, a woman of unlimited imagination and optimism whose friendship and support mean so much. Beth began planning the launch party for this book at her quilt shop in Amherst, Nova Scotia, as soon as she heard it was in the works—you are all invited. I know it will be spectacular!

Thank you to Hoffman California, Stof Fabrics, Mark Hordyszynski, and Michael Miller Fabrics for providing the beautiful materials used in these projects, all of which were designed using Electric Quilt® 7 software.

Last, but certainly not least:

THANK YOU American Quilter's Society for publishing this collection of rather oddball New York Beauty designs. I am forever grateful.

Contents

Introduction

My love affair with New York Beauty blocks began over a decade ago when I stitched my first one, and I have been hooked ever since. I've never met a New York Beauty quilt I didn't love. Whether you refer to this block by one of its other names, Rocky Mountain Road or Crown of Thorns, there is no mistaking the appeal; the contrast of spikes and curves is an exciting combination. Although I began with square blocks like everyone else, it soon became apparent that these beauties could just as easily be used to form round, semicircular, or quarter-round shapes—and thus the fun began!

Quilting Beauties Come in All Shapes & Sizes presents a fresh look and creative take on this versatile block; these are settings like you have never seen before. Bold, high-contrast colors and unusual outer shapes take the already elevated drama of a New York Beauty to an even higher level. The designs look complex but are in fact quite the opposite, often pairing the blocks with a simple Bowtie, Flying Geese, or a Double Four-Patch for amazing results. All of the projects in this collection are aimed at confident beginner-level quilters. Students in my workshops are always amazed at how easy it is to construct these stunning quilts.

This book of patterns and techniques uses foundation piecing to produce spiked arcs with perfect points and traditional piecing methods for sewing the curved seams. No special foot is required. The accompanying CD supplies printable full-size templates and foundations to make your cutting and sewing quick and easy.

Tips on pinning to keep the blocks "true" while sewing and instructions on how to make and apply bias binding to both inside and outside corners are provided. Included also are simple tricks to make the cutting lines match up perfectly when making continuous bias binding and a very easy method for joining the ends in a diagonal seam—things which puzzle many quilters. There are also tips on how to hang these unusual-shaped quilts. All the projects in *Quilting Beauties Come in All Shapes & Sizes* have been quilted on my domestic BERNINA 440.

Enjoy!

Karen Neary

General Directions

Please read these directions before beginning any projects.

Getting Started

Where to Start

All of the projects in this book are appropriate for confident beginner-level quilters. However, if you feel you'd like to warm up with the easiest of these quilts and build your skill level, the first project, X AND O, is a great place to start.

Templates and Foundations

Full-size patterns for each project are provided on the CD accompanying this book. They are grouped by project and are ready to print. Some are too large to fit on a single 8½" x 11" sheet of paper and will print on two pages. The printed registration marks will show you where to match the design edges. Tape the sheets together within the design area and you are ready to sew.

Seam Allowance

All of the projects in this book use ¼" for seam allowances.

Choosing Fabrics

Color and fabric selection is such a personal choice that I hesitate to offer suggestions in this area beyond saying that high contrast between the colors really amps up the drama of these quilt blocks. Try to avoid being too matchy-matchy when you choose a color family, and include as many relatives in that family tree as possible, even the black sheep.

As for prints, pretty much anything works in a New York Beauty with the exception of stripes or directional designs; save them for the binding as there is nothing prettier than a bias-cut stripe hugging the curved edge of a quilt.

Choose a small-scale print for the backgrounds under the spikes because your perfect points will not stand out nicely against a busy background. Instead, use the larger, busier prints for the centers or outer background pieces behind blocks. New York Beauty blocks are made more beautiful by using a wide variety of colors and prints, so let your imagination run wild when deciding.

Supplies

There really is not anything special you will need to complete the projects in this book. Regular quilting supplies such as rotary cutter and mat, ruler, pins, and scissors are all basic supplies. A lamp, light box, or other light source is also needed.

I like to use dollar store children's doodle pads for my foundation paper. They are cheap and the paper tears away easily after stitching. My printer has no problem with the thin newsprint sheets but some photocopiers have major issues feeding the paper through.

Clean and oil the sewing machine before you begin and insert a sharp needle for piecing. A ¼" foot is required to give consistent seam allowance results.

Because of the curved edges, the templates are cut using scissors; use your favorite method for this. I simply pin the paper template to the fabric (as in dressmaking), but you may choose to transfer the shapes to template material first and then trace them onto your fabric. Use whichever method gives you the best results.

The yardage provided for these quilts should be ample to complete each project. The calculation is based on a usable 40" width assumption. Cut all of the template pieces first and then use the leftovers for the foundation-pieced sections.

The backings, when pieced, are sewn with a vertical seam.

The battings and backings are cut 3" larger than the quilt top on all sides.

To prevent distortion, do not use steam when pressing the blocks.

Always use good quality thread in a color that matches the fabric. This is especially important when sewing the binding as these seams are pressed open; you do not want a contrasting thread color to be visible in the seam.

All of the projects in this book require bias binding to finish the curved edges, with the exception of X AND O and FLORENTINE which use straight-grain binding.

Using Templates

Templates are patterns for cutting the fabric shapes for the centers, outer backgrounds, bands, and other curved-design components of the blocks (Fig. 1). They have no numbered sections on them and are not meant to be sewn upon as you would do with a foundation. Some templates are marked to be cut with one edge along the fold of the fabric in order to provide you with full-size fabric pieces.

Print each project's full-size templates from the CD and cut them out. You will only need one copy of each template but if you find it more convenient to cut multiple fabric pieces with several templates, print as many copies as you wish. The cutting directions in each project will tell you how many pieces of fabric to cut from each template.

Making Paper Foundations

Foundations assist in piecing perfect points and spikes. They are marked with sewing lines which separate the numbered sections of the design and show where to place and sew the fabric pieces (Fig. 2). The cutting directions for each project will tell you how many foundations are needed. You can print them from the CD to easily and accurately make all of the paper foundations for each project.

Foundations which are too large to fit on an 8½" x 11" sheet of paper are divided into two sections. Piece both of them; then sew them together along the marked sewing line to complete the full-size pattern. Remove the paper carefully after they are sewn and staystitch along the curves to stabilize the bias.

Printing foundation copies directly from the CD is preferable to printing a master foundation and then using it to make additional copies on a photocopier. This is because some photocopiers will distort the image. If you decide to make foundation copies on a photocopier, it is wise to make one copy from the master and then check the size of the copy against the original before printing the rest of the copies.

If you have printed a single copy of a foundation, here is an easy alternative to a photocopier. Purchase a pad of newsprint in the children's art section of a dollar store (Fig. 3).

Tear out the number of sheets required for the pattern.

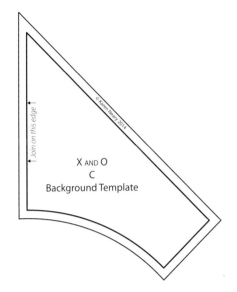

Fig. 1. Example of a template

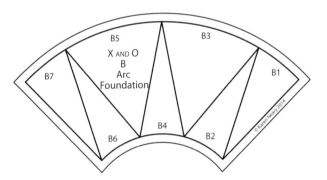

Fig. 2. Example of a foundation

Fig. 3

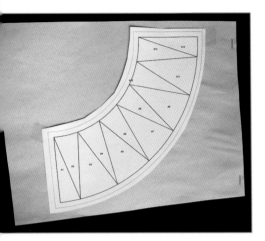

Fig. 4

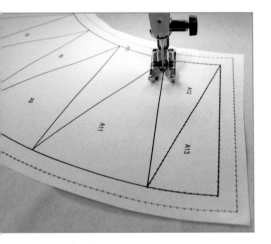

Fig. 5

Lay the master foundation on top of the newsprint sheets. Roughly cut around the master and tape the edges beyond the stitching lines in several places to keep them from moving. Staple the top edges of the sheets together while making sure there are no staples underneath the stitching lines on the master (Fig. 4).

Remove the thread from the sewing machine and put in an old needle. Stitch on all the marked lines, including the outer seam allowance (Fig. 5).

Carefully remove the master foundation. You now have a stack of foundations with the stitching lines all identically transferred. You can easily do eight foundations at a time using this method.

One big advantage with this method is that the lines are already scored making the paper-removal process easier once the fabrics are sewn together (Fig. 6).

Using a marker, number and label the foundation sections with the intended fabric colors (Fig. 7). This will save time in the long run as it helps prevent sewing the wrong fabric to a section.

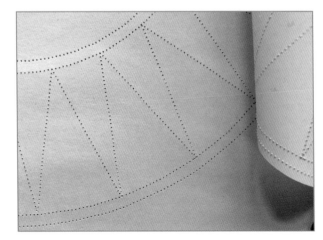

Fig. 6

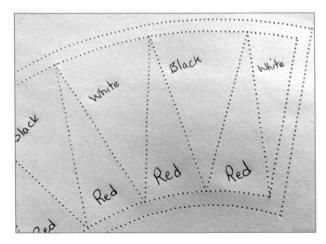

Fig. 7

How to Foundation Piece on Paper

Foundation piecing creates accurately and quickly pieced complex quilt blocks. All of the foundations in this book include a ¼" seam allowance around the completed piece. The seam allowance is shown on the foundations as a light thin line. The darker and heavier lines are the sewing lines.

The fabric pieces do not need to be cut precisely; each will be trimmed after it is stitched to the paper foundation. Make sure the pieces of fabric are at least ¼" larger on all sides than the section of the paper foundation that they will cover. Do not be concerned about fabric grain lines as the fabric is stabilized by the paper.

Scraps or strips of fabric work well for foundation piecing. The cutting directions in each project list the approximate size of the fabric pieces needed for the sections of the foundations. If you use scraps or strips, make sure they are at least as large as the approximate size given.

Set the sewing machine to a short stitch length of 12–16 stitches per inch.

There are many shapes which can be foundation pieced. The example below describes and illustrates the piecing of a New York Beauty arc (Fig. 8).

Hold a paper foundation up to a light source with the marked or right side of the paper facing you. Use the light coming through the back of the paper to help you see through the paper to align a piece of fabric over a section on the paper. This is shown as B1 in figure 9. The fabric is placed wrong sides together with the plain or back side of the paper foundation. Check to make sure that the fabric extends at least ¼" beyond the section of paper on all sides. Secure the fabric with a pin.

Place the fabric for the next section (shown as B2 in figure 10, page 14) right sides together with the first piece of fabric. Make sure the raw edge extends at least ¼" beyond the seam line between the first and second sections of the foundation.

Fig. 8. Diagram of a New York Beauty arc foundation

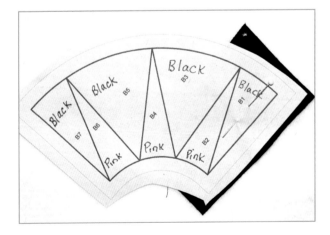

Fig. 9

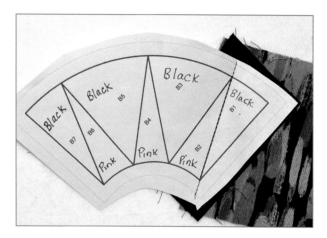

Fig. 10

Fig. 11

Fig. 12

With the marked side of the paper facing up and the two fabric pieces right sides together on the back of the paper, sew on the line between sections 1 and 2, beginning and ending a few stitches beyond the ends of the line (Fig. 10).

Fold the paper back along the sewn line and trim the seam allowance to ¼" (Fig. 11).

Flip the second fabric piece right-side out and press the two fabrics open. The pressed seam between them should be flat without tucks or folds.

Fold the paper back along the line between the second and third sections and trim the unsewn seam allowance of the second piece of fabric to ¼". Align a third fabric piece with right sides together with the trimmed edge of the second piece and stitch along the sewing line.

Continue adding fabric pieces on the foundation in numerical order until all of the sections are covered. Trim the block to size by cutting on the outside light thin line (Fig. 12).

Gently remove the paper foundation, being careful not to pull out any stitches.

After removing the paper, staystitch ⅛" from both curved edges of the arc; this step is important in preventing distortion when assembling the block.

Sewing the New York Beauty Block

The blocks in this book are of various shapes and sizes but the construction method is the same for all. It is helpful to lay out the block pieces before you sew (Fig. 13).

The photo illustrates the design of a 9" finished (9½" unfinished) block. A 9½" x 9½" area is outlined in green tape on a cutting mat. You can see that the foundation-pieced arc reaches to the 8" mark on the mat. Notice, also, that both curved edges of the arc have been staystitched to prevent distortion (Fig. 14).

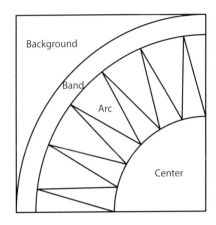

Fig. 13. Diagram of a New York Beauty block

Joining an Arc to a Center

Fold the bottom of the arc and either mark the center point with a pin or iron a small crease at that point. Fold the center in half and mark its center point (Fig. 15).

Match the center points of the arc and the center and pin them together (Fig. 16).

Pin the arc and the center together at each end of the seam (Fig. 17).

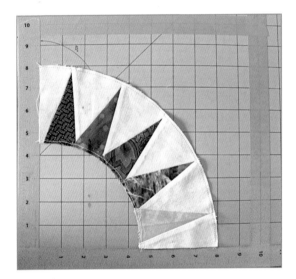

Fig. 14

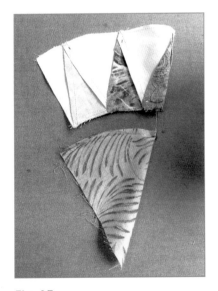

Fig. 15

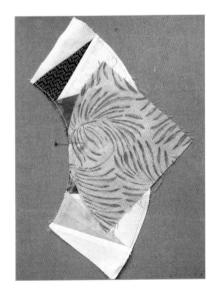

Fig. 16

Fig. 17

Fig. 18

Fig. 19

Fig. 20

Fig. 21

To prevent the edges of the block from pulling inward when you stitch the curve, pin the side of the arc to the side of the center (Fig. 18). You will not be sewing along this edge.

Insert a few additional pins along the arc and center seam. When the two are pinned together, it will look like the photo in figure 19. The red pins are holding the curved edges of the arc and center seam in place while the yellow-headed pins stabilize the sides. If you have a needle-down feature on your machine, it helps to keep the fabric from shifting while you sew the arc and center together.

Flip the piece over to the other side. Stitching from the opposite side has two advantages. The fullness is now on the top so you can see if you are stitching any tucks or pleats under the needle. Additionally, to make perfect points, you can see the seam where the spikes end so you know not to stitch into that area and lose the points of the spikes (Fig. 20). Stitch up to the pins and remove each one as you get to them.

Press the seam toward the center. Notice how straight the edges are, even without trimming (Fig. 21).

Joining an Arc to a Band or Outer Background

The arcs are sewn to bands or to outer backgrounds in the same manner as the arcs are sewn to the centers. First pin them together at the middle and at the ends of the curved stitching line. Then, pin them together along the sides to stabilize them. A New York Beauty block may have several curved rows of arcs and bands which are often completed by the addition of an outer background piece.

Shown are examples of an arc being sewn to a band. Notice the fullness is on the top for stitching (Figs. 22 and 23).

Press the band or background seam allowance away from the spikes to reduce the bulk. The edges of the block are straight and measure exactly 9½" (Fig. 24).

Fig. 22

Fig. 23

Fig. 24

How to Appliqué Tight Curves

Sometimes the curve of a seam is too steep to piece easily (Fig. 25, page 18). In this case, it is very simple to appliqué two pieces together on the curved edge.

First, cut out the fabrics as usual with the supplied templates. Trace the template of the piece to be appliquéd onto freezer paper, but do not add the seam allowance on the curved edge. Cut one piece of freezer paper for each fabric piece to be appliquéd.

Iron the shiny side of the freezer-paper template to the wrong side of the fabric pieces.

Rub glue stick on the fabric's seam allowances along the curved edges. Fold the fabric edges over the freezer-paper template and finger press (Fig. 26, page 18).

Overlap the edges of the two pieces to be joined by placing the piece to be appliquéd ¼" over the piece to be joined matching the seam lines. Pin into place (Fig. 27, page 18).

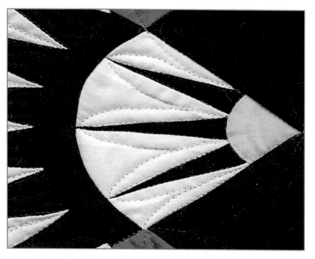

Fig. 25. An example of an appliquéd block with steep curves

Fig. 26

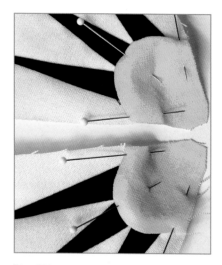

Fig. 27

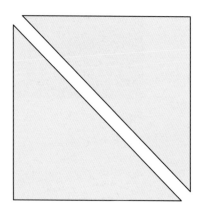

Fig. 28

Use invisible thread in the top of the machine and stitch using a short and narrow zigzag or blind hemstitch. Take care to catch only the edge of the freezer paper in the stitching. Gently remove the freezer paper from the back of the block. If the glue does not immediately release, place a damp cloth on the paper for a minute and then gently pull the paper away.

Making Continuous Bias Binding

For the projects in this book, a 20" square of fabric is used to make the bias binding.

Cut the square in half diagonally to form two triangles (Fig. 28).

Place the two triangles right sides together and stitch across the top edge. An easy way to remember the orientation of the two triangles is that the desired shape roughly resembles a pair of pants (Fig. 29).

When sewn together press the seam open. The result is a diamond shape.

On the wrong side of the fabric, draw parallel lines 2¼" apart diagonally across the seam. Along the two side edges, draw a registration line parallel to each end ¼" from the edge (shown in red in the diagram). These registration lines will allow perfect alignment of the seams and the cutting lines (Fig. 30).

With right sides facing, match the ends with the drawn lines together. Offset the drawn lines by one line by matching the first strip to the second strip. You may find it helpful to number both ends of the 2¼" strips to help you offset them. If you number them, write the numbers within the seam allowance so they will not show on the binding strips (Fig. 31).

Place pins straight through the registration and drawn lines in the seam allowance so the lines will match up when sewn (Fig. 32). This will seem wrong, but it isn't. Stitch and press the seam open.

Using scissors, begin at one end and cut along the lines to make one continuous strip of binding (Fig. 33).

Fold the long strips in half lengthwise with wrong sides together and press.

Machine stitch the bias binding to the quilt top and finish by hand sewing it to the back of the quilt.

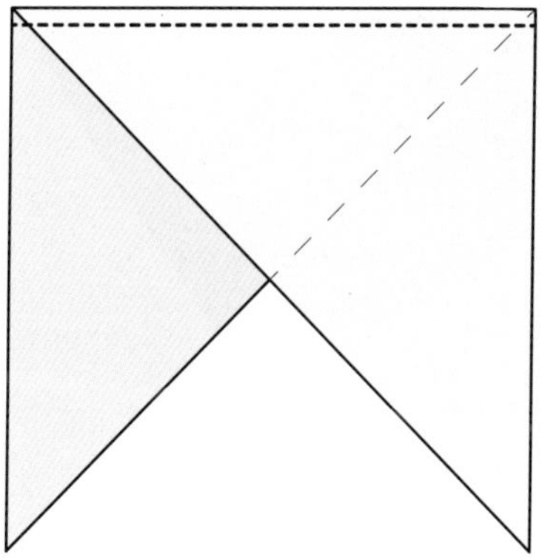

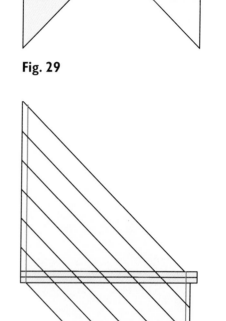

Fig. 29

Fig. 30

2¼"

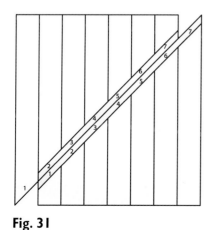

Fig. 31

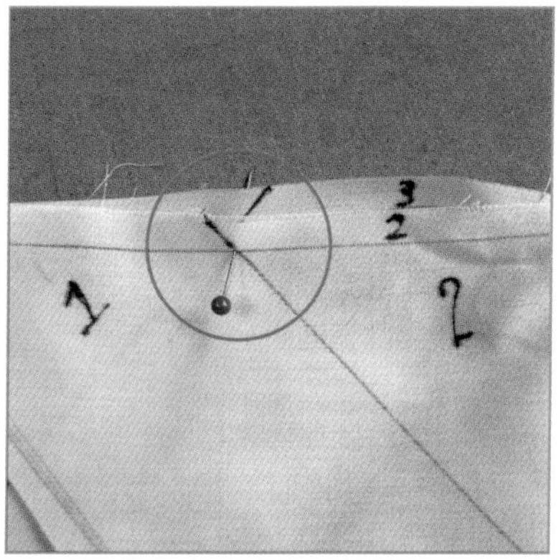

Fig. 32

Fig. 33

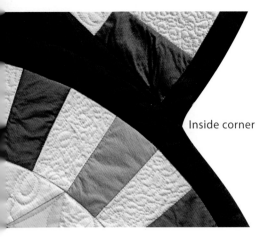

Inside corner

Fig. 34

Binding Inside and Outside Corners

Inside Corners (Fig. 34)

When applying binding to the inside corners, sew to the point where you will turn the corner. For the quilts in this book, sew to the seam line where the blocks intersect (Fig. 35).

Stop stitching and leave the needle in the down position (Fig. 36).

Lift the presser foot and turn the fabric so that the edge to be bound is in a straight line. As this happens, the fabric will bunch up in a point to the left of the needle. Smooth the binding so that it is perfectly flat and in a straight line (Fig. 37).

Resume machine stitching the binding around the quilt. When the binding is hand stitched to the back, there will be just enough fabric to fold it neatly down in the corner.

Fig. 35

Fig. 36

Fig. 37

Outside corner

Fig. 38

Outside Corners (Fig. 38)

Sew to within ¼" of the corner and lock the stitches. Clip the threads and fold the binding back so that it forms a 45-degree angle at the corner (Fig. 39).

Fold the binding forward over itself aligning its raw edge with the raw edge of the quilt. Begin stitching at the very end of the binding (Fig. 40).

Fig. 39

Fig. 40

Joining the Ends of the Binding

A diagonal seam is a great way to join the ends of binding. It distributes the bulk of seam and is an attractive finish.

Begin stitching the binding anywhere on the perimeter of the quilt, leaving a starting tail of about 6" of binding hanging free (Fig. 41).

Sew the binding around the quilt to within about 8" of where you began stitching (Fig. 42).

Bring the end tail of the binding up to meet where you started stitching the binding and cut it off (Figs. 43 and 44).

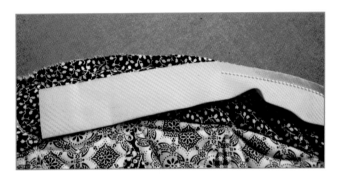

Fig. 41

Fig. 42

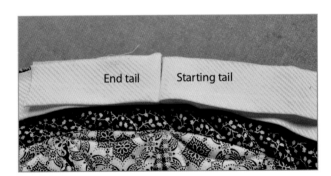

Fig. 43

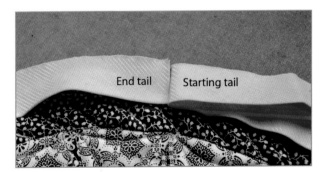

Fig. 44

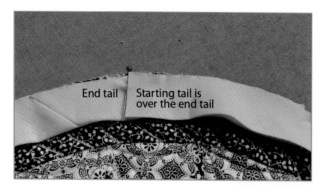

Fig. 45

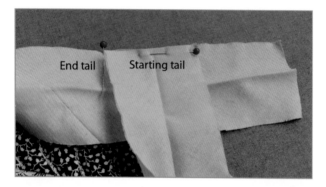

Fig. 46

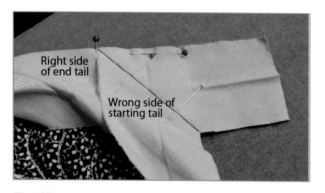

Fig. 47

Place the starting tail of the binding on top of the end tail. Cut the starting tail a couple of inches away from where you ended the stitching. If you cut it too close to the stitching you will have trouble sewing the binding seam. Leave yourself room to work.

Place a pin on the end tail at the cut edge of the starting tail (Fig. 45).

Lift the starting and the end tails. Open the folded binding ends. Make sure the right sides of the fabric are facing each other. Turn the starting tail toward you so that it is perpendicular (90 degrees) to the end tail. Place the left edge of the starting tail next to the pin mark on the end tail. Pin in place to hold (Fig. 46).

Mark a diagonal line across the wrong side of the starting tail from the upper left to the lower right corner and stitch along this line (Fig. 47).

Fold the binding back against the quilt edge to check for length. Trim the extra fabric from the seam allowance to ¼" (Fig. 48).

Stitch the finished binding to the remainder of the quilt edge (Fig. 49).

Fig. 48

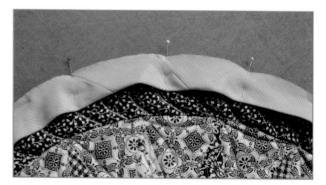

Fig. 49

QUILTING **Beauties Come in All Shapes & Sizes** — Karen Neary

Facing a Quilt

When you don't want binding to show on the front of the quilt, facing the edge is an easy way to give a clean finish. See the photo of my quilt TEMPUS FUGIT on page 52 which was faced rather than bound.

Prepare a bias facing as you would for binding. Sew the facing to the front of the quilt and join the ends in a diagonal seam. Instead of folding the facing to the back of the quilt so that half of it still shows on the front, like a binding does, fold the facing back on the stitching line. Press lightly. Turn the raw edge under ¼" and press. Secure the facing to the back of the quilt with hand stitches (Fig. 50). The facing is not seen on the front of the quilt.

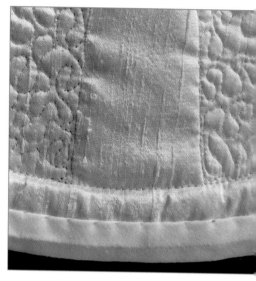

Fig. 50

How to Hang Unusual-Shaped Quilts

Hanging quilts of unusual shapes presents a challenge although not an impossible one. Sometimes you just have to get a bit creative with the laws of physics. First, decide which way is "up" for your quilt and then determine where you would like to place the hanging sleeve.

Try to pick a spot on the back of the quilt not too far from the top, preferably where the quilt begins to widen. If you place the sleeve too far down, the top of the quilt will flop forward. If it is too high up, the sides of the quilt may curl and not lie flat against the wall, thus requiring the addition of a second sleeve further down on the widest point of the quilt.

Measure the width of the quilt at the spot you have chosen and make a sleeve. There are excellent instructions on the American Quilter's Society website for making a hanging sleeve, found at http://quiltweek.com/contest.

Mark the vertical center of the quilt and place a ruler square on this mark to give a straight edge for the sleeve (Fig. 51).

Fig. 51. Aligning a hanging sleeve on the back of THISTLES IN THE HEATHER. The project for this quilt starts on page 44.

Fig. 52. A hanging sleeve is hand stitched to the back of Asian Beauty. The project for this quilt starts on page 38.

Fig. 53. A small ring is sewn to the back of Arabesque. The project for this quilt starts on page 79.

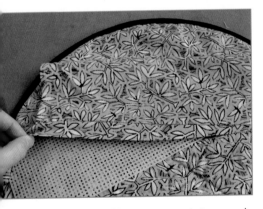

Fig. 54. Plastic canvas is inserted into a fabric pocket sewn to the back of Calliope. The project for this quilt starts on page 31.

Pin the sleeve in place (Fig. 52)

Hand stitch along both edges of the sleeve, and then insert a rod through it to hang the quilt.

If the quilt has a top point which persists in flopping forward, hand stitch a small ring to the top of the peak and hang the ring on a nail or hook in addition to the hanging sleeve (Fig. 53).

Some projects have a really unusual shape on the top edge and refuse to cooperate; such was Calliope. To stabilize this quilt, I made a pattern by tracing the outline of the top edge and drew a straight line for the bottom of the pattern. I folded a piece of fabric in half with wrong sides together, placed the bottom edge of the pattern along the fold to create a straight finished edge, and cut the pattern out.

The raw edges of the fabric were stitched in place on the back of the quilt along the top curved edge next to the binding. The bottom of the fabric, which was cut on a fold, created a straight-edged pocket into which stabilizer could be placed. The opening was then hand stitched closed once the stabilizer had been inserted.

The stabilizer you choose will depend on many things, including the size, weight, and the intended use of the quilt. A piece of cardboard works great but would need to be removed each time the piece is laundered. Plastic canvas makes a wonderful stabilizer to place in the pocket as it can be washed in the quilt (Fig. 54).

Instead of one hanging sleeve spanning the back of Calliope, I chose instead to make three shorter ones, each the width of the semicircle formed from the New York Beauty blocks. Under each sleeve is a pocket for plastic canvas to stabilize the top curves. There is a pocket on the side to support the partial New York Beauty that extends beyond the body of the quilt. A fifth stabilizer pocket was added to the quilt bottom to reinforce the lowest block and to ensure it hung straight (Fig. 55).

Fig. 55. Three hanging sleeves are sewn to the back of CALLIOPE in addition to five pockets for plastic canvas to help stabilize the edges of the quilt. See the diagram on page 37.

Projects

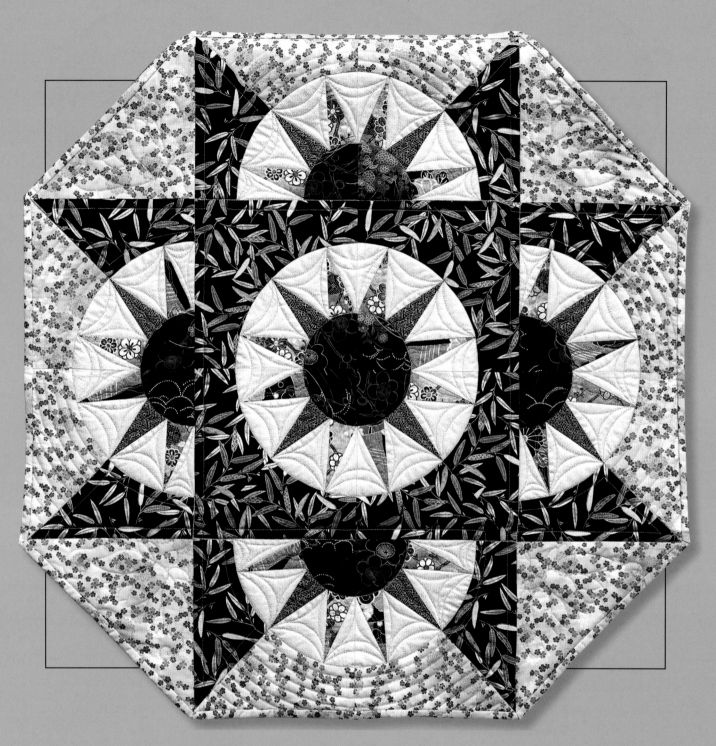

X AND O, 32" x 32". Designed, pieced, and quilted by Karen Neary.

X AND O

Splitting the background of the New York Beauty block creates a star pattern. High contrast prints work beautifully in this project.

Blocks (finished size)
(12) 8" x 8" New York Beauty

Fabrics and Supplies

1¼ yards   Cream and rose floral for the outer background, corners, and bias binding

½ yard   Burgundy floral for the centers

¾ yard   Black leaf print for the inner background

½ yard   Cream for the spike backgrounds

¾ yard   Assorted black-and-silver prints for the spikes

38" x 38"   Backing

38" x 38"   Batting

Quilt assembly diagram

X AND O and Maddie

Templates and Foundations

The following templates and foundations are full-size on the CD. Print the number of copies required for each.

A New York Beauty Center template. Make 1 copy.

B New York Beauty Arc foundation. Make 12 copies.

C New York Beauty Background template. Make 1 copy.

Cutting Directions

Cream and rose floral

✳ Fold the fabric in half and cut 4 background pairs using the C New York Beauty background template to make 4 left pieces and 4 right pieces.

✳ Cut (2) 9" x 9" squares. Subcut the squares in half diagonally to create (4) half-square triangles for the corners.

✳ Cut (1) 20" x 20" square for bias binding or (3) 2¼" x width-of-fabric strips for straight-grain binding.

Burgundy floral

✳ Cut 12 pieces using the A New York Beauty center template.

Black leaf print

✳ Fold the fabric in half and cut 8 background pairs using the C New York Beauty background template to make 8 left pieces and 8 right pieces.

Cream

✳ Cut 48 approximately 4" x 4" pieces for the B New York Beauty arc background sections.

Black-and-silver prints

✳ Cut 36 approximately 2" x 4" pieces for the B New York Beauty spikes.

Block Assembly

New York Beauty Blocks

Make 12 copies of the B New York Beauty arc foundation from the CD.

Foundation piece as instructed in the general directions beginning on page 13.

Use cream for the background and the assorted black-and-silver prints for the spikes. Alternate between the cream fabric for the odd-numbered sections and the black-and-silver prints for the even-numbered sections.

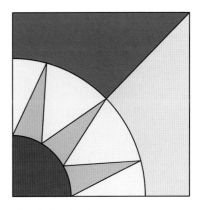

Fig. 1. Make 4.

Trim each block on the outside cutting line and carefully remove the paper foundation.

Sew the burgundy floral A New York Beauty centers to the small curved edge of each B arc. Press the seams toward the centers.

Referring to the C New York Beauty background template, locate the edge to be joined to its pair, then:

Fig. 2. Make 4.

✳ Lay out a black leaf print C background on the left and a cream and rose floral C background piece on the right. Sew them together at the joining line (Fig. 1). Make 4 sets.

✳ Lay out a cream and rose floral C background piece on the left and a black leaf print C background on the right. Sew them together at the joining line (Fig. 2). Make 4 sets.

✳ Lay out 2 black leaf print C inner backgrounds and match the joining edges. Sew them together at the joining line (Fig. 3). Make 4 sets.

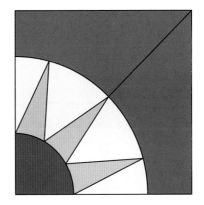

Fig. 3. Make 4.

Sew the joined C backgrounds to the large curved edge of each B arc. Press the seams toward the backgrounds.

Trim and square the blocks to 8½" x 8½".

Quilt Assembly

Lay out the blocks and the corner triangles in diagonal rows as shown in the assembly diagram on page 27 and sew them together. Press the seams to one side in alternate directions. Sew the rows together. Press the seams to one side.

Press the quilt top well.

Layer, baste, and quilt.

As there are no curved edges to bind, you may prefer to use a straight-grain binding by cutting (3) 2¼" x width-of-fabric strips. Sew them together on the short ends with a diagonal seam to make one long strip. Press the strip in half lengthwise and stitch it to the quilt top. Finish the binding by hand sewing it to the back of the quilt

To make and apply 2¼" bias binding from the 20" x 20" cream and rose floral fabric square, refer to the general directions on pages 18–22 for instructions.

LEFT: X AND O, detail. Full quilt on page 26.

CALLIOPE, 45" x 53".
Designed, pieced, and quilted by Karen Neary.

CALLIOPE

This very simple and fun quilt was created as a workshop sample to illustrate ways to hang an unusual-shaped quilt. It uses only two blocks and makes use of lots of colorful scraps.

Blocks (finished size)
(17) 7½" x 7½" New York Beauty
(18) 7½" x 7½" Bowtie

Fabrics and Supplies

Assorted scraps	(102) approximately 1¾" x 3¾" pieces for the New York Beauty spikes
	(50) approximately 5" x 6¾" pieces for the New York Beauty centers
	(6) approximately 6" x 12" pieces for the New York Beauty outer backgrounds
	(18) approximately 5" x 11" pieces for the bowties
⅛ yard each	17 assorted colors, solids, and small prints for the contrasting backgrounds for the arc
20" x 20" square	Black for bias binding
51" x 59"	Batting
51" x 59"	Backing

Quilt assembly diagram

Templates and Foundations

The following templates and foundations are full-size on the CD. Print the number of copies required for each.

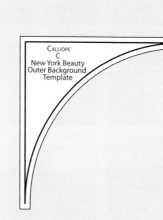

A New York Beauty Center template. Make 1 copy.

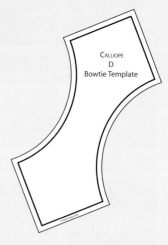

B New York Beauty Arc foundation. Make 17 copies.

C New York Beauty Outer Background template. Make 1 copy.

D Bowtie template. Make 1 copy.

Cutting Directions

5" x 6¾" scraps

✳ Cut 50 pieces using the A New York Beauty center template.

6" x 12" scraps

✳ Cut 6 pieces using the C New York Beauty outer background template.

5" x 11" scraps

✳ Cut 18 pieces using the D Bowtie template.

17 background fabrics

✳ Cut 7 approximately 2¾" x 3¾" pieces for the B New York Beauty arc background sections from each fabric. Keep the pieces from each background fabric together for ease in assembling the blocks.

Block Assembly

New York Beauty Blocks

Make 17 copies of the B New York Beauty arc foundation from the CD (Fig. 1).

Foundation piece as instructed in the general directions beginning on page 13.

Each of the 17 B arcs will have a different background fabric. For the B arc spikes, select scraps which contrast well with the background fabric.

Use the background fabric and the assorted 1¾" x 3¾" contrasting scraps for the spikes on the B arc foundation. Alternate between the background fabric for the odd-numbered sections and the scraps for the spikes for the even-numbered sections.

Trim each block on the outside cutting line and carefully remove the paper foundation.

Sew the A New York Beauty centers to the small curved edge of each B arc. Press the seams toward the A centers. Set the remaining A centers aside for now.

Sew a C New York Beauty outer background to the large curved edge of 6 of the B arc/A center units. Press the seams toward the C outer backgrounds. Make 6 blocks (Fig.2).

Trim and square the straight edges of each block to measure 8".

Bowtie Blocks

Sew an A New York Beauty center to both curved sides of 14 D bowties. Press the seams toward the bowties (Fig. 3). Set the remaining 4 D bowties aside for now.

Trim and square the straight edges of each block to measure 8".

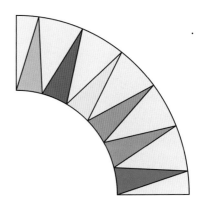

Fig. 1. Make 17.

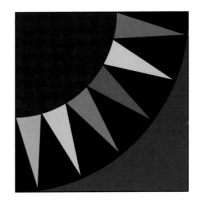

Fig. 2. Make 6.

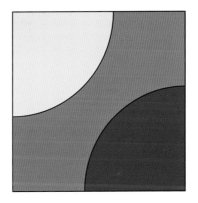

Fig. 3. Make 14.

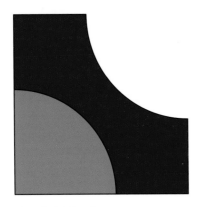

Fig. 4. Make 4.

Sew an A center to one curved side of the 4 remaining D bowties (Fig. 4). Press the seams toward the bowtie. Staystitch ⅛" from the edge of the open curves to stabilize these partial Bowtie blocks.

Trim and square the straight edges of each block to measure 8".

You will have 1 A center remaining. It will be used on the end of the fifth row when the quilt is assembled.

Quilt Assembly

Lay out blocks as shown in the quilt assembly diagram on page 33.

Join blocks together in rows. Press the seams in alternate directions in each row. Join the rows. Press the seams in one direction.

Press the quilt top well.

Layer, baste, and quilt paying particular attention to pinning around the circular opening in the quilt so it does not distort. Stitch ⅛" from the edge around the open circle to stabilize it.

Fig. 5. Trimming the quilt

When the project is quilted, use scissors and trim away the excess backing and batting around the edges and the circular opening (Fig. 5).

If you plan to make stabilizer pockets to help support the quilt, refer to the general directions on pages 23–25. CALLIOPE has 5 such pockets—3 at the top and 2 on the right side where the New York Beauty blocks curve outward from the quilt. Attach the pockets and insert plastic canvas cut to shape before binding the quilt to finish the curved edges.

This quilt also has 3 short hanging sleeves across the back of each New York Beauty block along the top of the quilt. Because of these curved edges, a long single sleeve will not work well. For information on hanging sleeves, please see the general directions on page 24.

Make and apply 2¼" bias binding from the 20" x 20" black fabric square. Refer to the general directions on pages 18–22 for instructions. Bind the opening in the quilt interior first and then bind the outside edges.

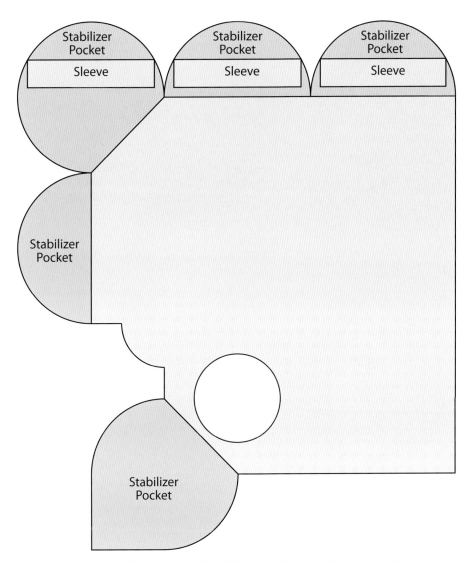

Fig. 6. The back of Calliope has 5 stabilizer pockets and 3 hanging sleeves.

ASIAN BEAUTY, 30" x 42½". Designed, pieced, and quilted by Karen Neary.

ASIAN BEAUTY

The New York Beauty blocks run up the sides of this quilt and are splayed like Oriental fans. They form a scalloped edging to the row of Double Four-Patch blocks which are set on-point in the center of the quilt. Feather quilting helps further define the graceful lines of the black arches.

Quilt assembly diagram

Blocks (finished size)
(12) 9" x 9" New York Beauty
(2) 9" x 9" Double Four-Patch

Fabrics and Supplies

¼ yard	Blue print for the New York Beauty inner bands
¾ yard	Assorted red prints for the New York Beauty spikes and Double Four-Patch squares
⅜ yard	Cream print for 6 New York Beauty backgrounds
⅜ yard	Gold print for 6 New York Beauty backgrounds
1¼ yards	Black for the New York Beauty outer bands and centers, Double Four-Patch squares, and bias binding
⅝ yard	Assorted tan prints for the New York Beauty backgrounds and Double Four-Patch squares
42" x 49"	Batting
42" x 49"	Backing

Templates and Foundations

The following templates and foundations are full-size on the CD. Print the number of copies required for each.

A New York Beauty Center template. Make 1 copy.

B New York Beauty Inner Band template. Make 1 copy.

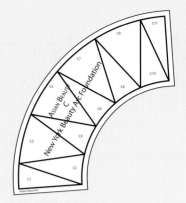

C New York Beauty Arc foundation. Make 12 copies.

D New York Beauty Outer Band template. Make 1 copy and tape the 2 pieces together.

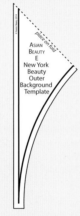

E New York Beauty Outer Background template. Make 1 copy and tape the 2 pieces together.

Cutting Directions

Blue print

✳ Cut 12 pieces using the B New York Beauty inner band template.

Assorted red prints

✳ Cut (8) 2¾" x 2¾" squares for the Double Four-Patch blocks.

✳ Cut 60 approximately 2" x 3¾" pieces for the C New York Beauty spikes.

Cream print

✳ Cut 36 approximately 3" x 3¾" pieces for the C New York Beauty background sections for 6 of the 12 arcs.

Gold print

✳ Cut 36 approximately 3" x 3¾" pieces for the C New York Beauty background sections for 6 of the 12 arcs.

Black

✳ Cut (1) 20" x 20" square for the binding.

✳ Fold the fabric wrong sides together. Place the D New York Beauty outer band template on the fold as marked and cut 12 pieces.

✳ Cut (8) 2¾" x 2¾" squares for the Double Four-Patch blocks.

✳ Cut 12 pieces using the A New York Beauty center template.

Assorted tan prints

✳ Fold the fabric wrong sides together. Place the E New York Beauty outer background on the fold as marked and cut 6 pieces.

✳ Cut (4) 5" x 5" squares for the Double Four-Patch blocks.

Fig. 1. Make 6.

Block Assembly

New York Beauty Blocks

Make 12 copies of the C New York Beauty arc foundation from the CD.

Foundation piece as instructed in the general directions beginning on page 13.

For 6 of the C arc foundations, use the cream background fabric with the assorted red prints for the spikes on the C arc foundation (Fig. 1). Alternate between the cream background fabric for the odd-numbered sections and the red scraps for the even-numbered sections.

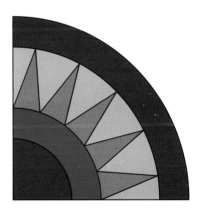

Fig. 2. Make 6.

For the other 6 C arc foundations, use the gold background fabric with the assorted red prints for the spikes on the C arc foundation (Fig. 2, page 41). Alternate between the gold background fabric for the odd-numbered sections and the red scraps for the even-numbered sections.

Trim each block on the outside cutting line and carefully remove the paper foundation.

Sew the black A New York Beauty centers to the small curved edge of each blue B New York Beauty inner band. Press the seams toward the A centers.

Sew the blue B inner bands to the small curved edge of each C arc. Press the seams toward the B inner bands.

Sew the C arcs to the small curved edge of each black D New York Beauty outer band. Press the seams toward the D outer bands.

Sew the 6 New York Beauty blocks with the cream print background under the spikes to the tan E New York Beauty outer background pieces. The 6 blocks with the gold background do not have E outer background pieces to make them square. These will be placed to create the rounded edges of the quilt.

Press the blocks flat. Trim and square the straight edges of the blocks to 9½".

ASIAN BEAUTY and Polly

Double Four-Patch Blocks

Sew the black and red 2¾" x 2¾" squares together in pairs. Press the seams toward the black squares (Fig. 3) Make 8 pairs.

Fig. 3

Join the pairs together alternating colors. Press the seams to one side (Fig. 4).

Make (4) 5" x 5" four-patch units.

Fig. 4

Sew the four-patch units to the 5" x 5" tan squares. Press the seams to one side.

Make 2 Double Four-Patch blocks (Fig. 5). Press the blocks flat, then trim and square them to 9½" x 9½".

Quilt Assembly

Lay out the blocks in diagonal rows as shown in the assembly diagram on page 39 and sew them together. Press the seams to one side in alternate directions.

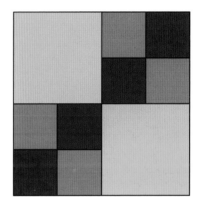

Fig. 5

Sew the rows together. Press the quilt top well.

Layer, baste, and quilt.

Make and apply 2¼" bias binding from the 20" x 20" black fabric square. Refer to the general directions on pages 18–22 for instructions.

THISTLES IN THE HEATHER, 27" x 34½". Designed, pieced, and quilted by Karen Neary.

THISTLES IN THE HEATHER

N ew York Beauty blocks resembling thistle blossoms with an overlaid argyle pattern give this piece a Scottish flair.

Blocks (finished size)
(4) 8" x 8" New York Beauty
(5) 8" x 8" Chain

Fabrics and Supplies

¾ yard	Dark purple for the short New York Beauty spikes and the Chain block backgrounds
1 yard	Light purple for the New York Beauty backgrounds, Chain blocks, outer backgrounds, and the binding
½ yard	Dark green for the New York Beauty centers and the Chain blocks
¼ yard	Light green for the Chain blocks
¼ yard	Medium green for the tall New York Beauty spikes
¼ yard	Brown-green for the New York Beauty backgrounds
33" x 41"	Backing
33" x 41"	Batting

Quilt assembly diagram

Templates and Foundations

The following templates and foundations are full-size on the CD. Print the number of copies required for each.

A New York Beauty Center template. Make 1 copy.

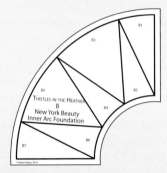

B New York Beauty Inner Arc foundation. Make 4 copies.

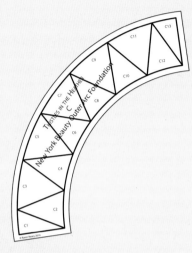

C New York Beauty Outer Arc foundation. Make 4 copies.

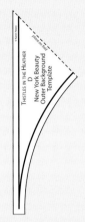

D New York Beauty Outer Background template. Make 1 copy and tape the 2 pieces together.

Cutting Directions

Dark purple

✳ Cut (2) 2½" x width-of-fabric strips. Subcut into (16) 2½" x 4½" rectangles for the Chain blocks.

✳ Cut (2) 1½" x width-of-fabric strips for the Chain blocks.

✳ Cut (1) 1½" x 26" strip for the Chain blocks.

✳ Cut 24 approximately 2¼" x 2¾" pieces for the C New York Beauty outer arc spikes or use scraps or strips.

Light purple

✳ Cut 2 pieces using the D New York Beauty outer background template.

✳ Cut 28 approximately 2¾" x 3" pieces for the C New York Beauty outer arc background sections or use scraps or strips.

✳ Cut (4) 2½" x 4½" rectangles for the Chain blocks.

✳ Cut (1) 1½" x 26" strip for the Chain blocks.

✳ Cut (1) 20" x 20" square for the binding.

Dark green

* ✳ Cut 4 pieces using the A New York Beauty center template.

* ✳ Cut (1) 1½" x width-of-fabric strip for the Chain blocks.

Light green

* ✳ Cut (1) 1½" x width-of-fabric strip for the Chain blocks.

* ✳ Cut (1) 1½" x 26" strip for the Chain blocks.

* ✳ Cut (1) 1½" x 26" strip for the Chain blocks.

Medium green

* ✳ Cut 12 approximately 2" x 4" pieces for the B New York Beauty inner arc spikes or use scraps or strips.

Brown-green

* ✳ Cut 16 approximately 4" x 4" pieces for the B New York Beauty inner arc background sections or use scraps or strips.

Block Assembly

New York Beauty Blocks (Figs. 1 and 2)

Make 4 copies each of the B New York Beauty inner arc foundation and the C New York Beauty outer arc foundation from the CD.

Foundation piece as instructed in the general directions beginning on page 13.

For the B inner arc foundations, use the approximately 4" x 4" pieces of the brown-green for the background fabric and the approximately 2" x 4" pieces of medium green fabric for the spikes. Alternate between the brown-green background fabric for the odd-numbered sections and the medium green fabric for the even-numbered sections.

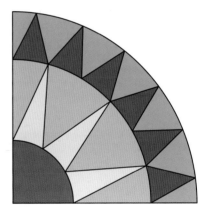

Fig. 1. Make 2.

Fig. 2. Make 2.

For the C outer arc foundations, use the approximately 2¾" x 3" pieces of the light purple for the background fabric and the approximately 2¼" x 2¾" pieces of dark purple fabric for the spikes. Alternate between the light purple background fabric for the odd-numbered sections and the dark purple fabric for the even-numbered sections.

Trim each block on the outside cutting line and carefully remove the paper foundation.

Sew the dark green A New York Beauty centers to the small curved edge of each B inner arc. Press seams toward the quarter circle.

Sew the C outer arcs to the large curved edge of each B inner arc. Press the seams toward the B inner arc.

Sew the 2 light purple D New York Beauty outer backgrounds to 2 of the New York Beauty blocks.

Chain Blocks

Sew a dark purple 1½" x width-of-fabric strip to the dark green 1½" x width-of-fabric strip to make a 2½" x width-of-fabric strip-set. Press the seam to one side. Subcut the strip-set into 22 1½" x 2½" pieced rectangles (Fig. 3).

Sew a dark purple 1½" x width-of-fabric strip to the light green 1½" x width-of-fabric strip to make a 2½" x width-of-fabric strip-set. Press the seams to one side. Subcut the strip-set into (26) 1½" x 2½" pieced rectangles (Fig. 4).

Sew the remaining dark purple 1½" x 26" strip to the light green 1½" x 26" strip to make a 2½" x 26" strip-set. Press the seams to one side. Subcut the strip-sets into (16) 1½" x 2½" pieced rectangles.

You will now have a total of 42 dark purple and light green 1½" x 2½" pieced rectangles.

Sew the light purple 1½" x 26" strip to the light green 1½" x 26" strip to make a 2½" x 26"

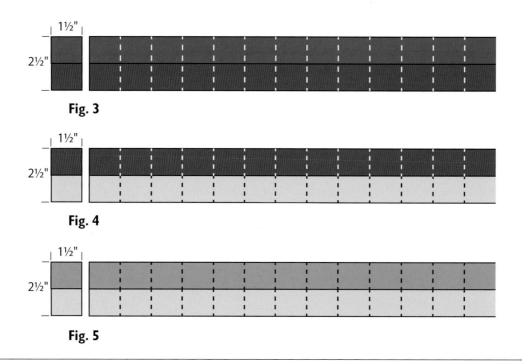

2½" | 1½"

Fig. 3

2½" | 1½"

Fig. 4

2½" | 1½"

Fig. 5

strip-set. Press the seam to one side. Subcut the strip-set into (16) 1½" x 2½" pieced rectangles (Fig. 5).

Sew (2) 1½" x 2½" dark purple and dark green pieced rectangles together to form a four-patch unit. Press the seam to one side. Make 6 units (Fig. 6).

Fig. 6. Make 6 units.

Sew (2) 1½" x 2½" dark purple and light green pieced rectangles together to form a four-patch unit. Press the seam to one side. Make 16 units (Fig. 7).

Fig. 7. Make 16 units.

Sew (2) 1½" x 2½" light purple and light green pieced rectangles together to form a four-patch unit. Press the seam to one side. Make 8 units (Fig. 8).

Fig. 8. Make 8 units.

Sew (1) 1½" x 2½" dark purple and dark green pieced rectangle to (1) 1½" x 2½" dark purple and light green pieced rectangle to form a four-patch unit. Press the seam to one side. Make 10 units (Fig. 9).

Fig. 9. Make 10 units.

Center Chain Block

To make the center Chain block, sew a dark purple and dark green four-patch unit to each end of a dark purple 2½" x 4½" rectangle piece. Make 2 (Fig. 10).

Fig. 10. Make 2.

Referring to figure 11, arrange 2 dark purple and dark green four-patch units and 2 dark purple/dark green/light green four-patch units. Add a dark purple 2½" x 4½" rectangle to 2 opposite sides (Fig. 12). Sew these units together. Make 1.

 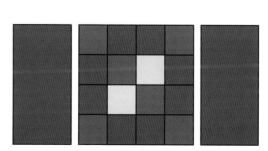

Fig. 11   **Fig. 12.** Make 1.

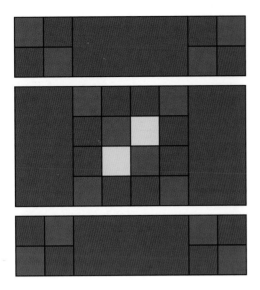

Fig. 13

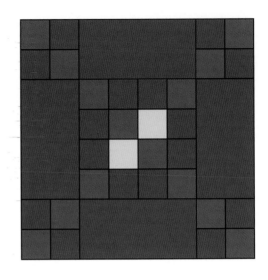

Fig. 14. Make 1 center block.

Sew the 2 strips shown in figure 10 to the top and bottom of the unit shown in figure 12. See figures 13 and 14.

Square the block to 8½" x 8½".

Fig. 15. Make 4.

Fig. 16. Make 4.

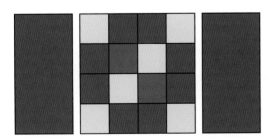

Fig. 17. Make 4.

Side Chain Blocks

Sew a dark purple and light green four-patch unit to each end of a dark purple 4½" x 2½" rectangle. Make 4 (Fig. 15).

Sew a light purple and light green four-patch unit to each end of a light purple 4½" x 2½" rectangle. Make 4 (Fig. 16).

Referring to figure 17, arrange 2 dark purple and light green four-patch units and 2 dark purple/dark green/light green four-patch units. Add a dark purple 2½" x 4½" rectangle to 2 opposite sides. Sew these units together. Make 4 (Fig. 17).

Sew the strip shown in figure 15 to the top of the unit shown in figure 17. Sew the strip shown in figure 16 to the bottom of this unit. Make 4 (Figs. 18 and 19).

Square the blocks to 8½" x 8½".

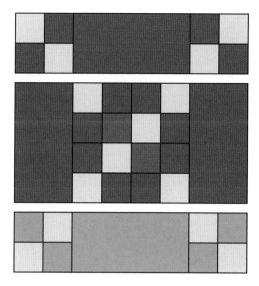

Fig. 18

Fig. 19. Make 4.

Quilt Assembly

Lay out the blocks in rows as shown in the assembly diagram on page 45 and sew them together. Press the seams to one side in alternate directions.

Sew the rows together. Press the quilt top well.

Layer, baste, and quilt.

Make and apply 2¼" bias binding from the 20" x 20" light purple fabric square. Refer to the general directions on pages 18–22 for instructions.

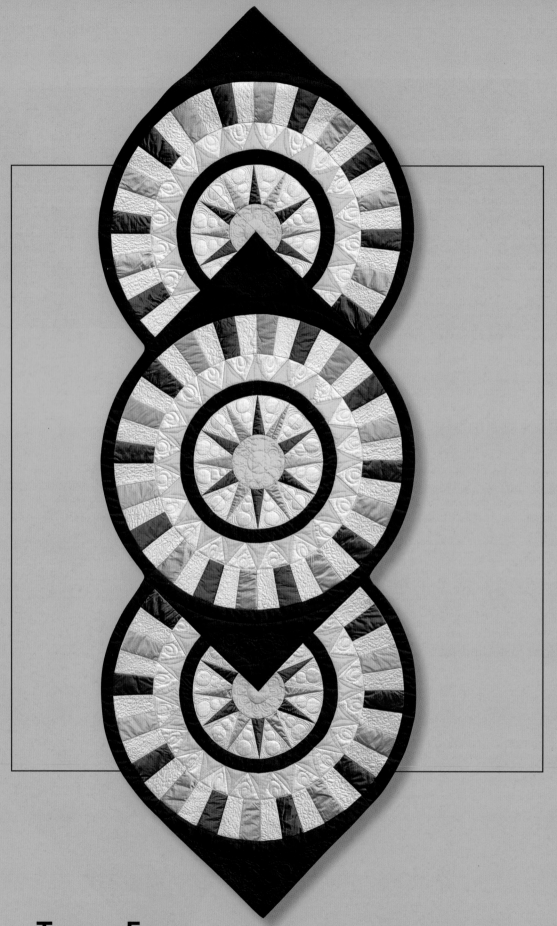

TEMPUS FUGIT, 24" x 66". Designed, pieced, and quilted by Karen Neary.

TEMPUS FUGIT

This beautiful wallhanging is pieced entirely from silk but would be just as lovely in cotton. The name *Tempus Fugit* is Latin for "time flies" and seemed appropriate as the blocks resemble the face of a clock. Instead of binding, the edges of this quilt are faced with a bias strip and hand stitched to the back.

Blocks (finished size)
(10) 12" x 12" New York Beauty

Fabrics and Supplies

½ yard	Light blue for the New York Beauty inner arc spikes and the New York Beauty outer arc rays
½ yard	Medium blue for the New York Beauty inner arc spikes and the outer arc rays
2 yards	Dark blue for the New York Beauty inner bands, New York Beauty outer bands, New York Beauty outer backgrounds, and the binding
1½ yards	Cream for the New York Beauty inner arc background, New York Beauty middle arc background, and the New York Beauty outer arc background rays
½ yard	Yellow for the New York Beauty centers and the New York Beauty middle arc spikes
30" x 72"	Backing
30" x 72"	Batting

* Instead of binding, this quilt can be faced with 1 package of purchased bias tape. If not using binding, you will only need 1⅝ yards of dark blue.

Quilt assembly diagram

Templates and Foundations

The following templates and foundations are full-size on the CD. Print the number of copies required for each.

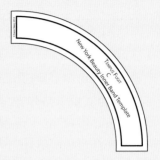

A New York Beauty Center template. Make 1 copy.

B New York Beauty Inner Arc foundation. Make 10 copies.

C New York Beauty Inner Band template. Make 1 copy.

D New York Beauty Middle Arc foundation. Make 10 copies.

E-1 New York Beauty Outer Arc foundation. Make 10 copies.

E-2 New York Beauty Outer Arc foundation. Make 10 copies.

F New York Beauty Outer Band template. Make 1 copy.

G New York Beauty Outer Background template. Make 1 copy.

Cutting Directions

Light blue

✳ Cut 14 approximately 1¾" x 3¾" pieces for the B New York Beauty inner arc spikes or use scraps or strips.

✳ Cut 24 approximately 2½" x 3¾" pieces for the E New York Beauty outer arc rays or use scraps or strips

Medium blue

✳ Cut 16 approximately 1¾" x 3¾" pieces for the B New York Beauty inner arc spikes or use scraps or strips

✳ Cut 26 approximately 2½" x 3¾" pieces for the E New York Beauty outer arc rays or use scraps or strips.

Dark blue

✳ Cut 10 pieces using the C New York Beauty inner band template.

✳ Fold the fabric wrong sides together. Place the F New York Beauty outer band template on the fold as marked and cut 10 pieces.

✳ Cut (1) 20" x 20" square for binding or purchase 1 package of bias binding and face the quilt.

✳ Fold the fabric wrong sides together. Place the G New York Beauty outer background template on the fold as marked and cut 4 pieces.

Cream

✳ Cut 40 approximately 3½" x 4" pieces for the B New York Beauty inner arc background sections or use scraps or strips.

✳ Cut 60 approximately 3" x 3½" pieces for the D New York Beauty middle arc background sections or use scraps or strips.

✳ Cut 50 approximately 2½" x 3¾" pieces for the E New York Beauty outer arc background rays or use scraps or strips.

Yellow

✳ Cut 10 pieces using the A New York Beauty center template.

✳ Cut 50 approximately 3" x 3½" pieces for the D New York Beauty middle arc spikes or use scraps or strips.

Fig. I

Fig. 2

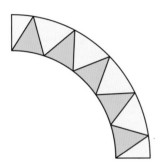

Fig. 3

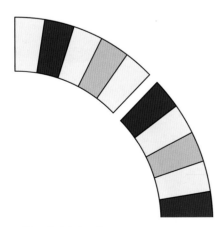

Fig. 4. Make 6.

Block Assembly

New York Beauty Blocks

Make 10 copies each of the B New York Beauty inner arc foundation, D New York Beauty middle arc foundation, and the E New York Beauty outer arc foundation from the CD.

Foundation piece as instructed in the general directions beginning on page 13.

For 6 of the B inner arc foundations, use the approximately 3½" x 4" pieces of cream for the background fabric and the approximately 1¾" x 3¾" pieces of medium blue and light blue fabrics for the spikes. Alternate between the cream background fabric for the odd-numbered sections; the medium blue fabric for the B2 and B6 spikes; and the light blue fabric for the B4 spikes (Fig. 1).

For 4 of the B inner arc foundations, use the approximately 3½" x 4" pieces of cream for the background fabric and the approximately 1¾" x 3¾" pieces of medium blue and 1¾" x 3¾" light blue fabrics for the spikes. Alternate between the cream background fabric for the odd-numbered sections; the light blue fabric for the B2 and B6 spikes; and the medium blue fabric for the B4 spikes (Fig. 2).

For the 10 D middle arc foundations, use the approximately 3" x 3½" pieces of cream for the background fabric and the approximately 3" x 3½" pieces of yellow fabric for the spikes. Alternate between the cream background fabric for the odd-numbered sections and the yellow fabric for the even-numbered spikes (Fig. 3).

The E New York Beauty outer arc foundation is printed as 2 pieces—E-1 and E-2. These will be sewn together after they are pieced.

For 6 of the E outer arcs use the approximately 2½" x 3¾" pieces of cream for the background rays and the approximately 2½" x 3¾" medium blue and light blue fabrics for the outer arc rays. Alternate between the cream background fabric for the odd-numbered sections; the medium blue fabric for the E2, E6, and the E10 rays; and the light blue fabric for the E4 and E8 rays (Fig. 4). Make 6 each of E-1 and E-2. Keep these separate from the E foundations in the next step.

For 4 of the E outer arcs use pieces of the cream for the background rays and the medium blue and light blue fabrics for the outer arc rays. Alternate between the cream background fabric for the odd-numbered sections; the light blue fabric for the E2, E 6, and the E 10 rays; and the medium blue fabric for the E4 and E8 rays (Fig. 5). Make 4 each of E-1 and E-2 rays.

Trim each foundation on the outside cutting line and carefully remove the paper foundation.

From the first set of 6 E-1 and E-2 arcs, pair an E-1 with an E-2 and sew them together between the sections marked as 5 and 6. Make 6 E-1/E-2 arcs which have 3 medium blue rays.

From the second set of 4 E-1 and E-2 arcs, pair and join them between the sections marked as 5 and 6 to make 4 E-1/E-2 arcs which have 3 light blue rays.

Sew the yellow A New York Beauty centers to the small curved edge of each B inner arc (Fig. 6). Press the seams toward the centers.

Sew the small curved edges of C New York Beauty inner bands to the large curved edge of each B inner arc (Fig. 7). Press the seams toward the C inner bands.

Sew the small curved edges of the D middle arcs to the large curved edge of each C inner band (Fig. 8). Press the seams toward the C inner bands.

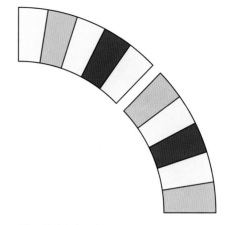

Fig. 5. Make 4.

Fig. 6

Fig. 7

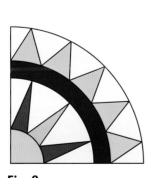

Fig. 8

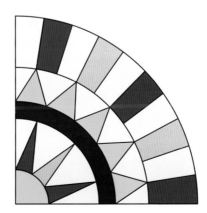

Fig. 9

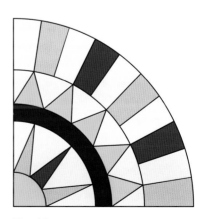

Fig. 10

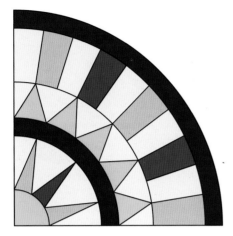

Fig. 11

Fig. 12. Make 4.

Pair the 6 A/B/C/D units that have 2 medium blue spikes in the B inner arc with the 6 E outer arcs that have 3 medium blue rays. Sew the small curved edges of the E outer arcs to the large curved edge of each D middle arc (Fig. 9, page 57). Press the seams toward the E outer arcs.

Pair the 4 A/B/C/D units that have 2 light blue spikes in the B inner arc with the 4 E outer arcs that have 3 light blue rays. Sew the small curved edges of the E outer arcs to the large curved edge of each D middle arc (Fig. 10, page 57). Press the seams toward the E outer arcs.

Sew the small curved edges of the F New York Beauty outer bands to the large curved edge of each E outer arc (Fig. 11). Press the seams toward the F outer bands.

To the 4 A/B/C/D/E/F units with the 2 light blue spikes in the B inner arc and the 3 light blue spikes in the E outer arc, sew the small curved edges of the G New York Beauty outer backgrounds to the large curved edge of the F outer bands (Fig. 12). Press the seams toward the F outer bands.

Square the straight edges of the blocks to 12½".

Quilt Assembly

Lay out the blocks as shown in the assembly diagram on page 53 and sew them together in diagonal rows. Press the seams to one side in alternate directions.

Sew the rows together. Press the quilt top well.

Layer, baste, and quilt.

Determine whether the quilt will be bound or faced.

For bias binding, make and apply 2¼" bias binding from the 20" x 20" dark blue fabric square. Refer to the general directions on pages 18–22 for instructions.

For a facing, purchase one package of bias binding and apply the facing following the general directions on page 23.

FLORENTINE, 34" x 39". Designed, pieced, and quilted by Karen Neary.

FLORENTINE

Elongated New York Beauty blocks circled by Flying Geese give lots of movement to this hexagonal show stopper.

Blocks (finished size)
(6) 9½" x 16½" New York Beauty
(6) 9½" x 16½" Flying Geese

Fabrics and Supplies

½ yard	Gold print 1 for the New York Beauty centers and the Flying Geese centers
1 yard	Gold print 2 for the backgrounds of 3 New York Beauty fans and the Flying Geese triangles
½ yard	Gold print 3 for the New York Beauty outer backgrounds
½ yard	Black floral for the New York Beauty outer backgrounds
1 yard	Brown for the backgrounds of 3 New York Beauty fans and the Flying Geese triangles
2 yards	Black solid for the New York Beauty spikes, Flying Geese background sections, Flying Geese outer backgrounds, and the straight grain binding
40" x 45"	Backing
40" x 45"	Batting

Quilt assembly diagram

Templates and Foundations

The following templates and foundations are full-size on the CD. Print the number of copies required for each.

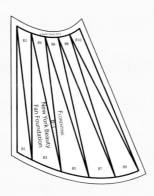

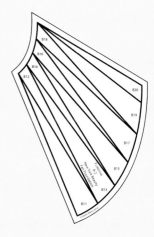

A New York Beauty Center template. Make 1 copy.

B-1 New York Beauty Fan foundation. Make 6 copies.

B-2 New York Beauty Fan foundation. Make 6 copies.

Templates and Foundations (continued)

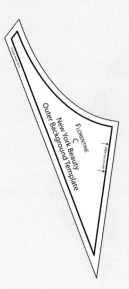

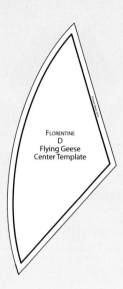

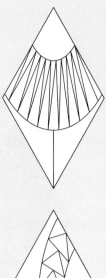

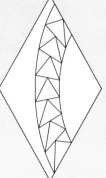

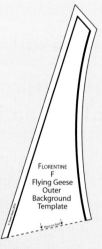

C New York Beauty Outer Background template. Make 1 copy.

D Flying Geese Center template. Make 1 copy.

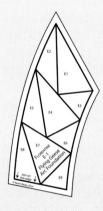

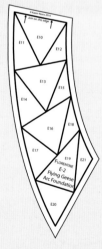

E-1 Flying Geese Arc foundation. Make 6 copies.

E-2 Flying Geese Arc foundation. Make 6 copies.

F Flying Geese Outer Background template. Make 1 copy.

Cutting Directions

Gold print 1

✳ Cut 6 pieces using the A New York Beauty center template.

✳ Cut 6 pieces using the D Flying Geese center template.

Gold print 2

✳ Cut 30 approximately 1¾" x 7½" pieces for 3 B-1/B-2 New York Beauty fan background sections.

✳ Cut 21 approximately 2½" x 3¾" pieces for the E-1/E-2 Flying Geese triangles.

Gold print 3

✳ Cut 6 pieces using the C New York Beauty outer background template from a single layer of fabric with the template placed right-side up on the wrong side of the fabric.

Black floral

✳ Cut 6 pieces using the C New York Beauty outer background template from a single layer of fabric with the template placed right-side up on the right side of the fabric.

Brown

✳ Cut 30 approximately 1¾" x 7½" pieces for 3 B-1/B-2 New York Beauty fan background sections.

✳ Cut 21 approximately 2½" x 3¾" pieces for the E-1/E-2 Flying Geese triangles.

Black solid

✳ Fold the fabric wrong sides together. Place the F Flying Geese outer background template on the fold as marked and cut 6 pieces.

✳ Cut 84 approximately 2½" x 3¾" pieces for the E-1/E-2 Flying Geese background sections.

✳ Cut 60 approximately 1¼" x 7½" pieces for the B New York Beauty fan spikes.

✳ Cut (4) 2¼" x width-of-fabric strips for the straight-grain binding.

Fig. 1. Make 3 with gold print 2 backgrounds.

Fig. 2. Make 3 with brown backgrounds.

Fig. 3. Make 6.

Fig. 4

Block Assembly

Make 6 copies each of the B-1 and B-2 New York Beauty Fan foundations and the E-1 and E-2 Flying Geese Arc foundations from the CD.

Foundation piece as instructed in the general directions beginning on page 13.

New York Beauty Blocks

For 3 of the B-1 and B-2 fan foundations, use the approximately 2" x 7½" pieces of gold print 2 fabric for the fan backgrounds and the approximately 1¼" x 7½" pieces of black solid fabric for the spikes. Alternate between the gold print 2 background fabric for the odd-numbered sections and the black solid fabric for the even-numbered sections.

Sew a B-1 foundation to a B-2 foundation joining the B10 section to the B11 section to make a complete fan. Make 3 B fans with gold print 2 backgrounds (Fig. 1).

For the other 3 B-1 and B-2 fan foundations, use the approximately 2" x 7½" pieces of brown fabric for the fan backgrounds and the approximately 1¼" x 7½" pieces of black solid fabric for the spikes. Alternate between the brown background fabric for the odd-numbered sections and the black solid fabric for the even-numbered sections.

Sew a B-1 foundation to a B-2 foundation joining the B10 section to the B11 section to make a complete fan. Make 3 B fans with brown backgrounds (Fig. 2).

Trim each fan foundation on the outside cutting line and carefully remove the paper foundation.

Join a C New York Beauty gold print 3 outer background and a C New York Beauty black floral background together along the center line. Make 6 pieced backgrounds (Fig. 3). Press the seams toward the black floral fabric.

Sew the C pieced backgrounds to the B fans (Fig. 4).

Sew the A New York Beauty gold print 1 centers to each fan (Fig. 5). Press the seams toward the A centers.

Measured side to side and top to bottom, these diamond-shaped New York Beauty blocks are 9½" wide and 16½" long.

Lay out 3 New York Beauty blocks together alternating 2 gold blocks and 1 brown block (Fig. 6).

The seams will be only partially sewn together at this point. Begin stitching the first 2 New York Beauty blocks together at the top of the point and sew the seam to within ¼" of the outside edge (Fig. 7).

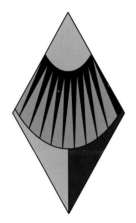

Fig. 5

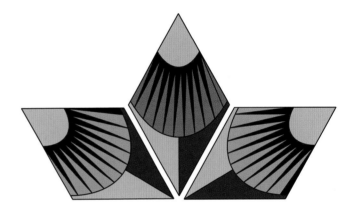

Fig. 6

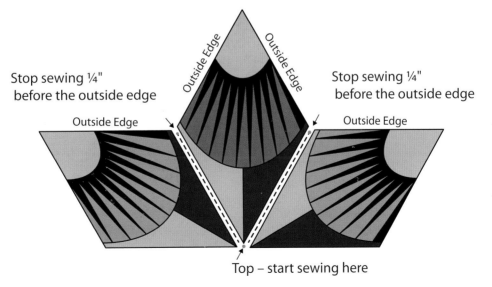

Stop sewing ¼" before the outside edge

Outside Edge

Outside Edge

Outside Edge

Outside Edge

Stop sewing ¼" before the outside edge

Outside Edge

Top – start sewing here

Fig 7. End the seam ¼" from the outside edge.

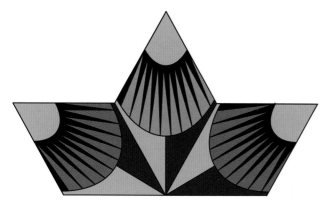

Fig. 8

Backstitch and end the seam. Press the seam open.

Add the second gold block on the right side of the brown block. Beginning at the center, stitch from the top to within ¼" of the outside edge (Fig. 7, page 65). Press the seam open.

Lay out and sew the remaining 3 New York Beauty blocks together alternating 2 brown blocks and 1 gold block (Fig. 8).

As with the previous set of 3 New York Beauty blocks, the seams are only partially sewn together at this point. Begin stitching the first 2 blocks together at the top of the point and sew the seam to within ¼" of the outside edge. Refer to figure 7, page 65.

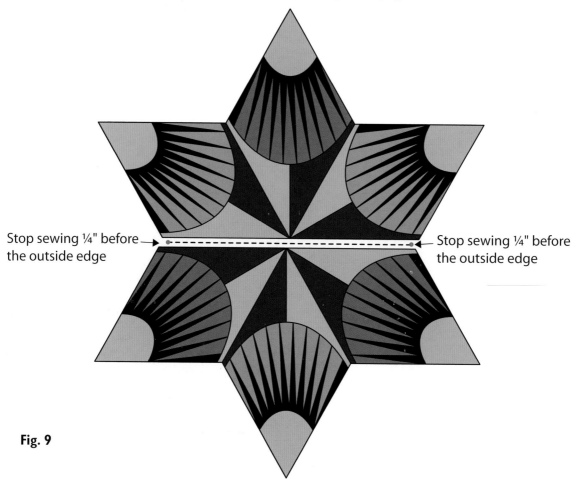

Stop sewing ¼" before the outside edge ⟶

⟵ Stop sewing ¼" before the outside edge

Fig. 9

Backstitch and end the seam. Press the seam open.

Add the second brown block on the right side of the gold block. Beginning at the center, stitch from the top to within ¼" of the outside edge (Fig. 8). Press the seam open.

Matching the centers and points, sew the 2 sets of New York Beauty units together beginning ¼" from the outside edge of 1 side and ending ¼" from the opposite outside edge (Fig. 9).

Press the center seam open (Fig. 10).

Fig. 10

Flying Geese Blocks

It is helpful to label the E-1 and E-2 Flying Geese arc foundation sections with the colors that will be sewn on them.

For 3 of the E-1 and E-2 foundations, the colors of the Flying Geese sections are as follows (Fig. 11):

Gold print 2: E1, E7, E13, and E19

Brown: E4, E10, and E16

Black: E2, E3, E5, E6, E8, E9, E11, E12, E14, E15, E17, E18, E 20, and E21

Trim each Flying Geese foundation on the outside cutting line and carefully remove the paper foundation.

Sew an E-1 foundation to an E-2 foundation joining the E8 and E9 sections to the E10 section to make a complete E arc. Make 3 E arcs that begin and end with gold print 2 geese (Fig. 12).

For the remaining (3) E-1 and E-2 Flying Geese arc foundations (Fig. 12), mark the sections as follows (Fig. 13):

Gold print 2: E4, E10, and E16

Brown: E1, E7, E13, and E19

Black: E2, E3, E5, E6, E8, E9, E11, E12, E14, E15, E17, E18, E 20, and E21

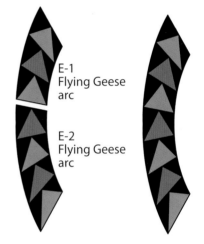

E-1
Flying Geese
arc

E-2
Flying Geese
arc

Fig. 11　　　　　**Fig. 12**

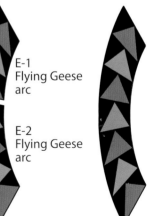

E-1
Flying Geese
arc

E-2
Flying Geese
arc

Fig. 13　　　　　**Fig. 14**

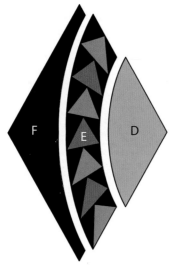

Fig. 15

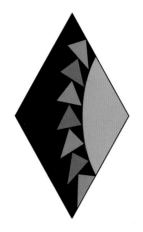

Fig. 16

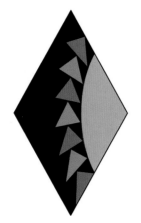

Fig. 17

Trim each Flying Geese foundation on the outside cutting line and carefully remove the paper foundation.

Sew an E-1 foundation to an E-2 foundation joining the E8 and E9 sections to the E10 section to make a complete E arc. Make 3 E arcs that begin and end with brown geese (Fig. 14, page 67).

Sew the curved edge of the D Flying Geese centers to the small inner curve of each arc. Press the seams toward the centers.

Sew the F Flying Geese outer backgrounds to the E arcs by matching the curved edge of the background to the large outer curve of the arc (Fig. 15). Press the seams toward the backgrounds.

You will have 3 blocks beginning and ending with gold Flying Geese triangles (Fig. 16) and 3 beginning and ending with brown Flying Geese triangles (Fig. 17.)

Measured from side to side and top to bottom, these diamond-shaped Flying Geese blocks are 9½" wide and 16½" long.

Quilt Assembly

Position a Flying Geese block between 2 New York Beauty blocks and pin along one side. Working from the center outward, begin stitching ¼" from the center seam and sew to the outer edge of the block (Fig. 18). This step will allow you room to pivot to stitch the second side without creating a pucker.

Align the remaining side of the Flying Geese block with the second New York Beauty block and pin into place. Again, begin the stitching ¼" from the center end of the seam and stitch to the outer edge.

Press the seams toward the Flying Geese block. The Y seam should lie flat with the point of the center matching the center seam of the New York Beauty blocks (Fig. 19).

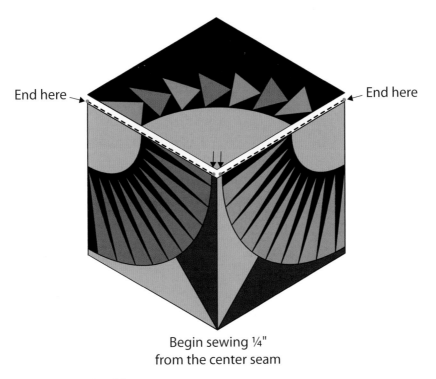

End here →

← End here

Begin sewing ¼"
from the center seam

Fig. 18

Sew the remaining Flying Geese blocks between the New York Beauty blocks to finish the top.

Press the quilt top well.

Layer, baste, and quilt.

When the quilting is complete, trim and straighten the edges of the quilt.

Using the black binding strips, prepare and apply the binding following the general directions on pages 18–22.

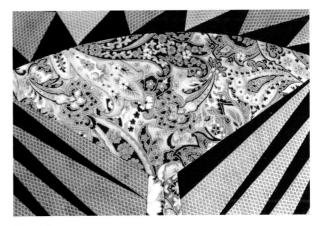

Fig. 19

OSTENTATION, 30½" x 36". Designed, pieced, and quilted by Karen Neary.

OSTENTATION

The name for a flock of peacocks is an *ostentation*, and it aptly describes this showy quilt. Palm blocks are encircled by New York Beauty blocks to form this stunning design. The yellow centers of the New York Beauty blocks are reminiscent of the eye on a peacock's tail feathers. A beaded black tassel is added to the bottom and a shiny black button draws your eye to the center of the quilt. OSTENTATION is quilted in various feather designs using a gold metallic thread.

Blocks (finished size)
(6) 8¾" x 15½" New York Beauty
(6) 8¾" x 15½" Palm

Fabrics and Supplies

½ yard	Teal blue small print (Fabric 1) for the Palm background
¼ yard	Aqua blue small print (Fabric 2) for New York Beauty pieced spikes
½ yard	Teal and gold print (Fabric 3) for the New York Beauty background
⅜ yard	Royal blue and black print (Fabric 4) for the New York Beauty middle band and pieced spikes
1¾ yards	Black and gold small print (Fabric 5) for the Palm leaves, New York Beauty inner and outer bands, pieced spikes, outer backgrounds, and the binding
⅜ yard	Medium teal print (Fabric 6) for the Palm leaves
¼ yard	Gold texture (Fabric 7) for the Palm leaves and the New York Beauty centers and pieced spikes
37" x 42"	Backing
37" x 42"	Batting
1" Black button	
Black tassel	

RIGHT: Quilt assembly diagram

OSTENTATION uses fabrics like these:

Fabric 1

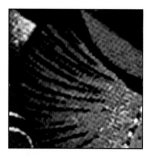

Fabric 2

Fabric 3

Fabric 4

Fabric 5

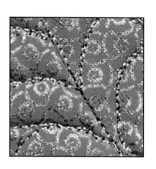

Fabric 6

Fabric 7

Templates and Foundations

The following templates and foundations are full-size on the CD. Print the number of copies required for each.

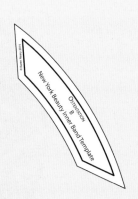

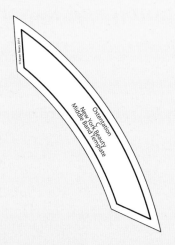

A New York Beauty Center template. Make 1 copy.

B New York Beauty Inner Band template. Make 1 copy.

C New York Beauty Middle Band template. Make 1 copy.

D-1 New York Beauty Arc foundation. Make 6 copies.

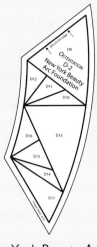

D-2 New York Beauty Arc foundation. Make 6 copies.

E New York Beauty Outer Band foundation. Make 1 copy.

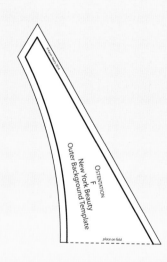

F New York Beauty Outer Background template. Make 1 copy.

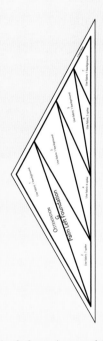

G Palm Left foundation. Make 6 copies.

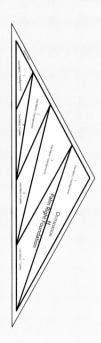

H Palm Right foundation. Make 6 copies.

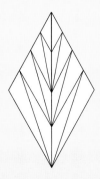

Cutting Directions

Dark teal and blue print (Fabric 1)

✳ Cut (5) 2¾" x length of fabric strips for the backgrounds of the G Palm Left foundation and the H Palm Right foundation.

Dark aqua and blue print (Fabric 2)

✳ Cut 24 approximately 2" x 2½" pieces for the D New York Beauty arc D4, D8, D12, and D16 inner sections of the pieced spikes.

Teal and gold print (Fabric 3)

✳ Cut 30 approximately 4¼" x 4½" pieces for the D York Beauty arc D1, D5, D9, D13, and D17 backgrounds.

Royal blue and black print (Fabric 4)

✳ Cut 6 pieces using the C New York Beauty middle band template.

✳ Cut 24 approximately 2" x 2¼" pieces for the D New York Beauty arc D3, D7, D11, and D15 middle sections of the pieced spikes.

Black and gold print (Fabric 5)

✳ Cut 12 approximately 1½" x 6¾" pieces for the G Palm Left foundation and the H Palm Right foundation.

✳ Cut a 20" x 20" square for the bias binding.

✳ Cut 6 pieces using the B New York Beauty inner band template.

✳ Fold the fabric wrong sides together. Place the E New York Beauty outer band template on the fold as marked and cut 6 pieces.

✳ Fold the fabric wrong sides together. Place the F New York Beauty outer background template on the fold as marked and cut 2 pieces.

✳ Cut 12 approximately 1½" x 2" pieces for the D New York Beauty arc D6 and D14 alternating outer points of the pieced spikes.

Medium teal print (Fabric 6)

✳ Cut 12 approximately 2¼" x 9" pieces for the G Palm Left foundation and the H Palm Right foundation.

Gold texture (Fabric 7)

✳ Cut 12 approximately 2" x 11" pieces for the G Palm Left foundation and the H Palm Right foundation.

✳ Cut 6 pieces using the A New York Beauty center template.

✳ Cut 12 approximately 1½" x 2" pieces for the D New York Beauty arc D2 and D10 alternating outer points of the pieced spikes.

Block Assembly

Make 6 copies each of the D New York Beauty arc foundation, the G Palm Left foundation, and the H Palm Right foundation from the CD.

Foundation piece as instructed in the general directions beginning on page 13.

New York Beauty Blocks

While appearing complex, this block is actually easy and fun to sew. The key is to pay close attention to the numbered order marked on the foundation on which 6 fabrics are sewn together for this arc.

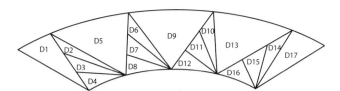

Fig. 1

Using the D-1 and D-2 New York Beauty arc foundations, start with a D1 background piece and add a D2 piece. Add a D3 piece and continue sewing in order until the arc is completed. As you sew, compare figures 1 and 2 with your work to help develop the design correctly (Figs. 1 and 2).

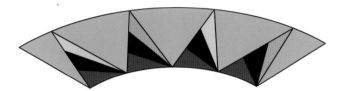

Fig. 2

Trim each arc on the outside cutting line and carefully remove the paper foundation.

Pair a D-1 arc with a D-2 arc and sew them together to join the D6 section to the D9 section. Press the seam toward the D9 section. Make 6 D-1/D-2 arcs.

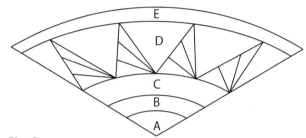

Fig. 3

Lay out a block using an a New York Beauty center, a B New York Beauty inner band, a C New York Beauty middle band, a D-1/D-2 arc, and an E New York Beauty outer band (Fig. 3). Sew them together.

Press the seam between the A center and the B inner band toward the A center. Press the seam between the B inner band and the C middle band toward the B band. Press the seam between the C middle band and the D-1/D-2 arc toward the C middle band. Press the seam between the D-1/D-2 arc and the E outer band toward the E outer band. Make 6 blocks (Fig. 4).

Fig. 4

Add the F New York Beauty outer backgrounds to 2 of the arcs (Fig. 5). These blocks will be used at the top and the bottom of the quilt.

Fig. 5

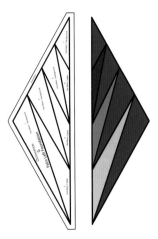

Palm Blocks

Like the New York Beauty block, these blocks are also easy and fun to sew. Pay close attention to the numbered order and the fabrics marked on each section of the foundations.

The background sections of the G Palm Left foundation and the H Palm Right foundation are pieced from the 2¾" x width of fabric strips. Sew a strip to the foundation and cut it to the length necessary for covering that section of the foundation. This will save you time by eliminating cutting many small pieces of the background fabric.

Fig. 6 (left). The G Palm Left foundation

Fig. 7 (right). The completed left side of the Palm block.

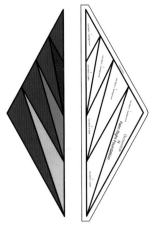

Fig. 8 (left). The completed right side of the Palm block.

Fig. 9 (right). The H Palm Right foundation

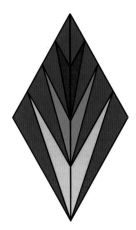

Fig. 10

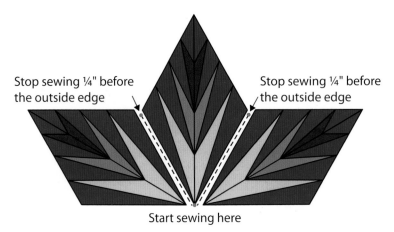

Stop sewing ¼" before the outside edge

Stop sewing ¼" before the outside edge

Start sewing here

Fig. 11. End the seam ¼" from the outside edge.

Using the G Palm Left foundation, start with background piece 1 and sew a spike piece 2 to it. Continue sewing in numerical order, alternating backgrounds and spikes until the palm is completed. As you sew, compare figures 6 and 7 with your work to help develop the design correctly.

Repeat the step above using the H Palm Right foundation while referring to figures 8 and 9.

Sew the left and right halves of a Palm block together in the center (Fig. 10). Press the seams to one side. Make 6 blocks.

Quilt Assembly

Lay out the Palm blocks into 2 sets of 3 (Fig. 11).

The seams are only partially sewn together at this point. Begin stitching the first 2 blocks of 1 set together at the center and sew the seam to within ¼" of the outside edge as shown in figure 11.

Fig. 12

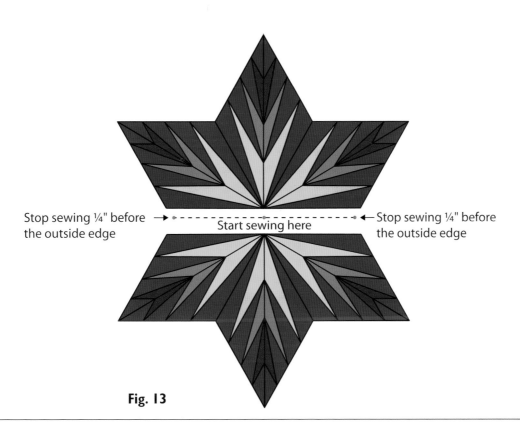

Stop sewing ¼" before the outside edge →   Start sewing here   ← Stop sewing ¼" before the outside edge

Fig. 13

Backstitch and end the seam. Press the seam open.

Join the third block to the set by beginning stitching at the center and end ¼" from the outside edge (Fig. 12, page 77).

Sew the second set of 3 blocks together, beginning at the center and ending each seam ¼" from the outside edge.

Join the 2 sections across the center by beginning and ending the stitches ¼" from the ends (Fig. 13, page 77). Press the seam open.

Fig. 14. Begin sewing the seam ¼" from the center seam.

Position a New York Beauty block in the intersection between 2 Palm blocks and pin along one side. Working from the center outward, begin stitching ¼" from the center seam and sew to the outer edge of the block (Fig. 14). This step will allow you room to pivot to stitch the second side without creating a pucker.

Align the remaining side of the New York Beauty block with the second Palm block and pin into place. Again, begin the stitching ¼" from the center end of the seam and stitch to the outer edge.

Press the seams toward the New York Beauty block. The Y seam should lie flat with the point of the center matching the center seam of the Palm blocks.

Add the remaining 5 New York Beauty blocks between the points of the Palm blocks. Make sure to sew the 2 New York Beauty blocks with the black and gold outer backgrounds to opposite sides of the quilt as shown on the quilt assembly diagram on page 71.

Press the quilt top well.

Layer, baste, and quilt.

When the quilting is complete, trim and straighten the edges of the quilt.

Make and apply 2¼" bias binding from the 20" x 20" black and gold (Fabric 5) fabric square. Refer to the general directions on pages 18–22 for instructions.

Sew the button to the quilt center and hand stitch the tassel to the bottom point.

ARABESQUE, 14½" x 36". Designed, pieced, and quilted by Karen Neary.

ARABESQUE

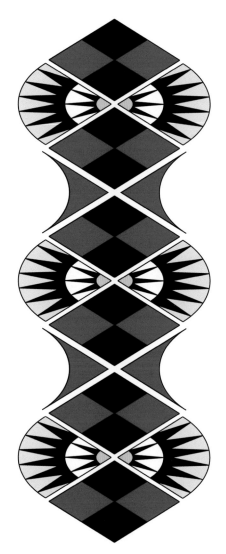

Quilt assembly diagram

Use your imagination when choosing fabrics for this funky hanging or table topper. The yellow centers of the New York Beauty blocks resemble a cat's eyes...or maybe you see a diamondback python?

Blocks (finished size)
(6) 5¾" x 6¹³⁄₁₆" New York Beauty
(6) 5¾" x 9⅝" Four-Patch Diamond

Fabrics and Supplies

½ yard   Red for Four-Patch diamonds and backgrounds

1¼ yards   Black for New York Beauty spikes and bands, Four-Patch diamonds, and the binding

¼ yard   White for New York Beauty inner arc backgrounds

½ yard   Gray for New York Beauty outer arc backgrounds

12" x 12"   Yellow for the New York Beauty centers

40" x 18"   Backing

40" x 18"   Batting

12" x 12"   Freezer paper

Invisible thread

Templates and Foundations

The following templates and foundations are full-size on the CD. Print the number of copies required for each.

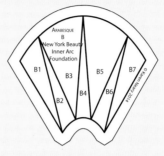

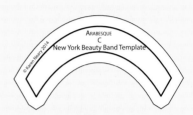

A New York Beauty Center template. Make 1 copy.

B New York Beauty Inner Arc foundation. Make 6 copies.

C New York Beauty Band template. Make 1 copy.

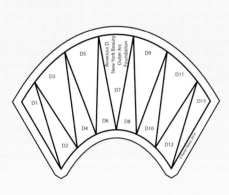

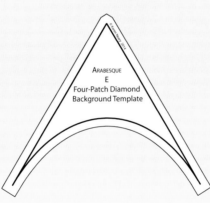

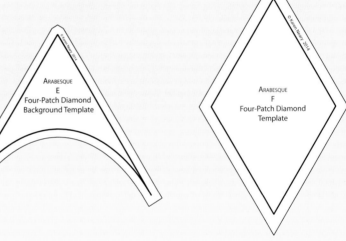

D New York Beauty Outer Arc foundation. Make 6 copies.

E Four-Patch Diamond Background template. Make 1 copy.

F Four-Patch Diamond template. Make 1 copy.

Cutting Directions

Red

✳ Cut 4 pieces using the E Four-Patch Diamond outer background template.

✳ Cut 12 pieces using the F Four-Patch Diamond template.

Black

✳ Cut (1) 20" x 20" square for bias binding.

✳ Cut 12 pieces using the F Four-Patch Diamond template.

✳ Cut 6 pieces using the C New York Beauty band template.

✳ Cut 18 approximately 1" x 2¾" pieces for the B New York Beauty inner arc B2, B4, and B6 spikes.

✳ Cut 36 approximately 1¼" x 3¾" pieces for the D New York Beauty outer arc D2, D4, D6, D8, D10, and D12 spikes.

White

✳ Cut 24 approximately 1¾" x 2¾" pieces for the B New York Beauty inner arc B1, B3, B 5, and B7 background sections.

Gray

✳ Cut 42 approximately 1¾" x 3¾" pieces for the D New York Beauty outer arc D1, D3, D5, D7, D9, D11, and D13 background sections.

Yellow

✳ Cut 6 pieces using the A New York Beauty center template.

Block Assembly

Make 6 copies each of the B New York Beauty inner arc foundation and the D New York Beauty outer arc foundation from the CD.

Foundation piece as instructed in the general directions beginning on page 13.

New York Beauty Blocks

For a B inner arc, use the approximately 1¾" x 2¾" pieces of white fabric for the arc backgrounds and the approximately 1" x 2¾" pieces of black for the spikes. Alternate between the white background fabric for the odd-number sections and the black fabric for the even-numbered sections. See figure 1. Make 6.

For a D outer arc, use the approximately 1¾" x 3¾" pieces of gray fabric for the arc backgrounds and the approximately 1¼" x 3¾" pieces of black for the spikes. Alternate between the gray background fabric for the odd-number sections and the black fabric for the even-numbered sections. See figure 2. Make 6.

Trim the B inner arcs and the D outer arcs on the outside cutting lines and carefully remove the paper foundations.

Staystitch ⅛" from the curved edges of each arc.

Because of the steep curved seams in this block, the sections have been appliquéd as

Fig. 1. Make 6.

Fig. 2. Make 6.

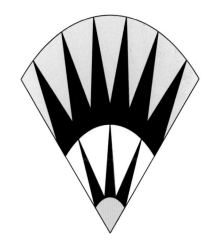

Fig. 3.

instructed in the general directions on pages 17–18. Join an A New York Beauty center to the small curve of a B inner arc. Join this arc to the small curve of a C New York Beauty band which in turn is sewn to the small curve of a D outer arc.

Assemble 6 blocks (Fig. 3).

Fig. 4

Four-Patch Diamond Blocks

Sew the F Four-Patch Diamond pieces together in pairs of 1 red and 1 black (Fig. 4). Press the seam toward the black piece. Make 12 pairs.

Flip 6 of the red and black pairs (Fig. 5).

Fig. 5

Sew 2 pairs of red and black diamonds together in sections (Fig 6). Make 6 Four-Patch Diamond blocks. The blocks are 5½" measured side to side in the direction indicated by the arrow below.

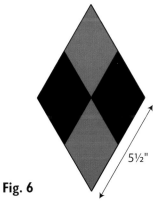

Fig. 6

5½"

Fig. 7

Fig. 8

Quilt Assembly

Sew a New York Beauty block to a Four-Patch Diamond block (Fig. 7). Make 6 units.

Staystitch the curved edges of the 4 red E Four-Patch Diamond outer backgrounds to prevent stretching while sewing.

Sew an E outer background to a Four-Patch Diamond block (Fig. 8). Make 4 units. Press the seams to one side.

Arrange the 6 units as shown in figure 9 and sew them together.

Press the quilt top well.

Layer, baste, and quilt.

When the quilting is complete, trim and straighten the edges of the quilt.

Make and apply 2¼" bias binding from the 20" x 20" black fabric square. Refer to the general directions on pages 18–22 for instructions.

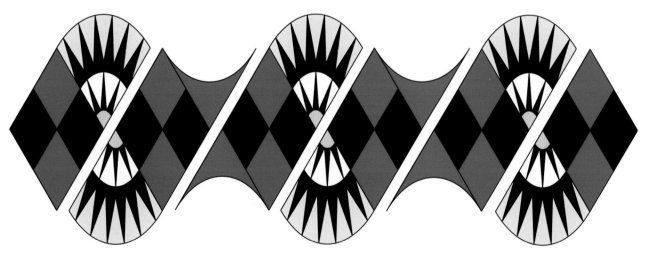

Fig. 9

BATIK BEAUTY, 48" x 48". Designed, pieced, and quilted by Karen Neary.

BATIK BEAUTY

s it a New York Beauty or not? The appearance says so with the quarter-center circle and the spiky band but the construction is similar to a Fan block. Regardless, it is too pretty not to include. This stunner is equally spectacular on a table or a wall.

Blocks (finished size)
(24) 8" x 8" New York Beauty

Fabrics and Supplies

1 yard	Aqua for the New York Beauty pieced spikes
1¼ yards	Blue for the New York Beauty pieced spikes
¾ yard	Dark orange for the New York Beauty outer backgrounds
½ yard	Light orange for the New York Beauty pieced spikes
¼ yard	Yellow for the New York Beauty centers
1¾ yards	Pale cream for the New York Beauty pieced spikes
1¾ yards	Black for the New York Beauty pieced spikes and the binding
54" x 54"	Backing
54" x 54"	Batting

Quilt assembly diagram

Templates and Foundations

The following templates and foundations are full-size on the CD. Print the number of copies required for each.

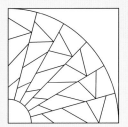

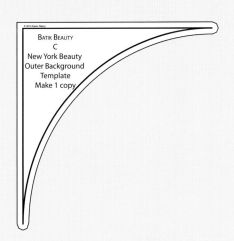

A New York Beauty Center template. Make 1 copy.

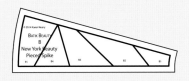

B New York Beauty Pieced Spike foundation. Make 144 copies.

C New York Beauty Outer Background Template. Make 1 copy.

Cutting Directions

Aqua

✳ Cut 144 approximately 2¼" x 2½" pieces for the B New York Beauty pieced spike B4 sections.

Blue

✳ Cut 144 approximately 2¼" x 2¾" pieces for the B New York Beauty pieced spike B3 sections.

Dark Orange

✳ Cut 12 pieces using the C New York Beauty outer background template.

Light Orange

✳ Cut 144 approximately 1½" x 2½" pieces for the B New York Beauty pieced spike B1 sections.

Yellow

✳ Cut 24 pieces using the A New York Beauty center template.

Pale cream

✳ Cut 144 approximately 3¼" x 3½" pieces for the B New York Beauty pieced spike B2 sections.

Black

✳ Cut (2) 20" x 20" squares for the bias binding.

✳ Cut 144 approximately 2¼" x 2¾" pieces for the B New York Beauty pieced spikes B5 sections.

Block Assembly

Fig. 1

Make 144 copies of the B New York Beauty pieced spike foundation from the CD.

Foundation piece as instructed in the general directions beginning on page 13.

New York Beauty Blocks

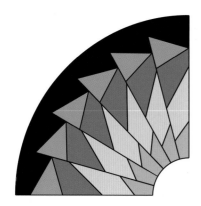

Fig. 2

For the B pieced spikes, foundation piece using the following colors in this order (Fig. 1):

B1 Light orange

B2 Pale Cream

B3 Blue

B4 Aqua

B5 Black

Make 144 pieced spikes.

Trim the B pieced spikes on the outside cutting lines. Leave the paper on for now.

Sew (6) B pieced spikes together (Fig. 2). Make 24 units.

Remove the paper and press the seams to one side.

Fig. 3

Sew a yellow A New York Beauty center to each pieced spike unit (Fig. 3). Press the seam toward the center.

Sew the dark orange C New York Beauty outer backgrounds to 12 pieced spike units (Fig. 4). The remaining 12 blocks do not have a background section.

Quilt Assembly

Lay out blocks as shown in the quilt assembly diagram on page 86.

Sew the blocks together in rows. Press the seams in the rows in alternate directions.

Join the rows. Press the seams to one side.

Press the quilt top well.

Layer, baste, and quilt.

When the quilting is complete, trim and straighten the edges of the quilt.

Make and apply 2¼" bias binding from the (2) 20" x 20" black fabric squares. Refer to the general directions on pages 18–22 for instructions.

Fig. 4

Gallery of Quilts

QUILTING **Beauties** Come in All Shapes & Sizes — Karen Neary

ABOVE: FARRAGO. 41½" x 41½". Designed, pieced, and quilted by Karen Neary. FARRAGO was a semifinalist in the New York State of Mind exhibit at the Fennimore Art Museum in Cooperstown, New York, in November 2010, and a semifinalist at the American Quilter's Society 2011 Paducah show. It was also chosen for the International Quilt Festival's traveling exhibit, O Canada 2012.

RIGHT: FARRAGO. 41½" x 41½". Designed, pieced, and quilted by Karen Neary.

OPPOSITE: NEW YORK, NEW YORK. 58" x 78". Designed, pieced, and quilted by Karen Neary.

GALLERY PHOTOS: KAREN NEARY

ABOVE: THE BEAUTY OF CHRISTMAS. 44" x 44". Designed, pieced, and quilted by Karen Neary.

ABOVE RIGHT: ROUNDABOUT AGAIN. 31" x 50". Designed, pieced, and quilted by Karen Neary.

RIGHT: ROUNDABOUT AGAIN. 31" x 50". Designed, pieced, and quilted by Karen Neary. This dramatic beauty was a semifinalist at AQS QuiltWeek® — Paducah, Kentucky 2013.

ABOVE: MARITIME BEAUTY. 30" x 30". Designed, pieced, and quilted by Karen Neary.

RIGHT: Student version of ROUNDABOUT AGAIN. 31" x 50". Designed by Karen Neary. Pieced and quilted by Joan Tufts of Saulnierville, Nova Scotia.

FAR RIGHT: Student version of ROUNDABOUT AGAIN. 31" x 50". Designed by Karen Neary. Pieced and quilted by Alisa Aymar of Meteghan, Nova Scotia.

GALLERY PHOTOS: KAREN NEARY

Resources

Fabrics

Hoffman California Fabrics, www.hoffmanfabrics.com

Mark Hordyszynski, http://madhatterofmaui.blogspot.com

Michael Miller Fabrics, http://www.michaelmillerfabrics.com

Stof Fabrics, http://www.stof-dk.com

Quilt Shop

Mrs. Pugsley's Emporium Inc., 50 East Victoria Street, Amherst, Nova Scotia, B4H 1X6 Phone: 902-661-4260, http://mrspugsleysemporium.ca/ (website), http://mrspsamherst.blogspot.ca/ (blog)

ORIENTAL BEAUTY. 32" x 32". Designed, pieced, and quilted by Karen Neary.

other AQS books

This is only a small selection of the books available from the American Quilter's Society. AQS books are known worldwide for timely topics, clear writing, beautiful color photos, and accurate illustrations and patterns. The following books are available from your local bookseller, quilt shop, or public library.

#1550. . . . . $24.95

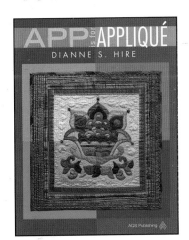

#1419. . . . . $24.95

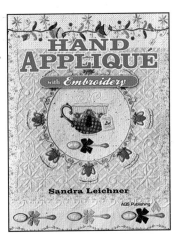

#8244. . . . . $26.95

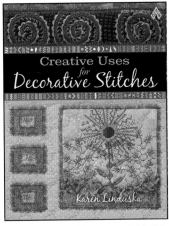

#8762. . . . . $24.95

#8681. . . . . $26.95

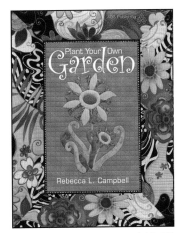

#1583. . . . . $12.95

#1586. . . . . $12.95

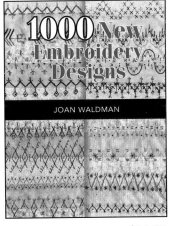

#8238. . . . . $26.95

#1644. . . . . $24.95

About the Author

Karen Neary has worked as a professional quilt designer since 1989. Her quilts have been featured in numerous magazines including *American Quilter*, *Quilters Newsletter*, *McCall's Quilting*, *Quilter's Connection*, and *The Canadian Quilter*. For 12 years, Karen penned a regular column for *Quick & Easy Quilting* magazine.

She has contributed to over a dozen books and co-authored *Canadian Heritage Quilting*. Her quilts have been exhibited across Canada and the United States, as well as in Japan and France. Karen's proudest accomplishment is designing and making a quilt which was presented to Sir Paul McCartney to commemorate his visit to Nova Scotia.

While her particular love is New York Beauty quilts, Karen also designs and stitches liturgical hangings and vestments. She enjoys teaching workshops and helping her husband with his beekeeping.

Karen is a graduate of the Bachelor of Arts and Bachelor of Education programs at Mount Allison University. She is a member of the Mayflower Quilters' Guild of Nova Scotia, the Canadian Quilters' Association, and an honorary member of La Guilde Acadienne de Clare.

Hailing from Five Islands, Karen currently resides in Amherst, Nova Scotia, Canada, with her husband, Jamie, and two sons, Patrick and Peter. The household also includes Polly and Maddie, two felines who offer input into all of Karen's quilting.

For more information please visit Karen's website and blog: karenneary.ca

KAREN NEARY

ASIAN BEAUTY and Polly